Value Education for Young Leaders

Value Education for Young Leaders
Nurturing the roots for a strong foundation

Hari Krishna Padavala

PARTRIDGE
A Penguin Random House Company

Copyright © 2015 by Hari Krishna Padavala.

ISBN: Hardcover   978-1-4828-5000-0
             Softcover   978-1-4828-5001-7
             eBook   978-1-4828-4999-8

Print information available on the last page.

To order additional copies of this book, contact
Partridge India
000 800 10062 62
orders.india@partridgepublishing.com

www.partridgepublishing.com/india

In this book titled "Value Education for Young Leaders", the author expertly narrates the advantages of imbibing moral and ethical values in students of higher education. Through his experience in academia and interactions with students, the author aptly brings in the important aspects of stress management and time management thus addressing self-empowerment and principles of leadership. Overall this book could be a great addition to modern educational system, where moral education practically stops at high school. I would recommend this book for all young, bright and energetic students out there who want to improve not just their qualifications but their character.

Dr. Ramana Kumar Vinjamuri, Assistant Professor
CBBE, Stevens Institute of Technology, New Jersey USA

Human mankind takes pride in its so called technical advancement, while it is plagued by the uncontrolled emotions of anger, lust, fear, stress and depression especially by the young generation leading to a kind of violence, which was never experienced hitherto. The present book on Value Education for Young Leaders presents a deep insight into the possible ways of vanquishing these enemies of the so called modern society and shows the path for a happy and peaceful life based on some spiritual facts.

Prof. (Dr.) R.M. Jalnekar, Director,
Viswakarma Institute of Technology, Pune, India

In Value Education for Young Leaders, the author points out the general problems faced by the present day young professional students and provide wonderful proven solution to the problem. Surely this is very useful book for all the students.

Dr. Deva Pratap, Prof. & Head, Civil engineering department,
National Institute of Technology, Warangal, India

This book on Value Education for Young Leaders is truly a valuable reference for all the student community to combat the challenges not only in young age but also will be useful throughout their life.
Dr. K. Hima Bindu, Associate Professor,
Kakatiya Medical College, Warangal, India

This book talks about conquering real enemies, enemies common to every human being, those enemies who otherwise seem to be unconquerable.
M. V. Srikanth, Manager, HPCL, Secunderabad, India

FOREWORD

In nature, we have different types of soils and out of them; clay is special in terms of its benefits to human mankind. The clayey soil is soft, supple and it can be moulded into any shape. When this soil is crafted by an expert sculptor it can turn into a master piece. Every student is like impressionable clay and when the student is moulded during his education in correct direction through habits and behaviour, surely he will become a good human being.

After the child is born, he grows and learns many things from his parents, relatives, friends and other members of society. Above all students spend significant period during education – the school, college or university plays an important role in contributing to the moral upbringing of the child. Thus, the author designed this book with valuable principles for young students to read, understand, contemplate and adopt them during their educational stage to become good leaders in the society.

When we compare human being with a tree, then youth will be like a tender plant. When we nurture the tender plant in right direction, a beautiful tree grows. We can characterize a good tree by its strong roots (similar to the good foundation of a building) similarly we can characterize a good student by the values, morals and ethics. At this juncture, I recall a statement by Albert Einstein saying "Try not to become a man of success but rather to become a man of values"

This book on value education for young leaders is compilation of wide variety of disciplinary topics which are very much useful to the entire student community in the world. As Dean of research and distinguished professor at University of Texas, Arlington, I am delighted to recommend this book for all the student fraternity who wish to become successful leaders in their family, profession, society and nation at large.

Dr. Anand J Puppala, P.E., F.ASCE, D.G.E.
Associate Dean of Research, College of Engineering
Distinguished Professor, Department of Civil Engineering
The University of Texas at Arlington, Arlington, USA

CONTENTS

PREFACE

For present students teaching is no longer in fashion because learning is their prime motto. This book is a learning resource for those who wish to be successful leaders in their student, professional and family life. This book on "**Value education for the young leaders**" is a student centred one and contents were arrived by conducting a survey with the students of National Institute of Technology, Warangal, India to have their view point and hence will help in the personality development of students.

Value education primarily deals with leading people towards perfection by taking into account their physical, emotional, intellectual and social needs. Corruption, terrorism, nepotism etc have become routine news in today's media. Scholars and leaders emphasize *Value based education is the solution to solve such type of problems.* At this stage a question arises: *don't most people already know right from wrong?* Yes, they know - but feel that they will fare better in life without following some of the basic moral codes.

Living by moral principles is like following traffic rules for smooth and safe travel. The main purpose of travel is not to follow traffic rules but to reach destination safely. If a traveller feels that traffic rules delay his journey or obstruct his reaching the destination then he may break them, if he thinks he can get away without any problem. Similarly, moral principles promote orderliness in our lives to reach our final destination. But modern education system, doesn't teach about the goal of social transactions or of the life itself. Consequently, people may stay moral out of deference to the culture or tradition, but give up morality when circumstances threaten or tempt them.

Many academicians in the field of technical education are feeling the need for imparting values, ethics and morals in modern education. As today's society has deviated from the good concepts of life, it is facing many calamities. A need is thus felt to revive a collective understanding of value based principles into the educational system, which will help the intelligent and energetic student community to be good leaders in the society.

Being the faculty of a professional institute for more than 2 decades and being the faculty in-charge for Centre for Value education for more than 3 years, I felt that there is a necessity to present the essential material on value based education from the perspective of imparting success into the lives of students. This book is essentially meant for those intelligent and energetic students who wish to identify their correct aspirations and to find out the methods to fulfil them with the theme of "**Adding values to life**". Many times, students are not in a position to clearly understand the basic necessities to become good leaders in their life and hence, this book is intended to provide the real valuables and ethics for proper behaviour in society along with leading a happy and peaceful life.

The goal of this book is to present the basics of value based educational system along with its necessity. If you visualize yourself as successful, who could lead a satisfactory life and could inspire people around you to know the secrets of satisfactory life - What type of information you will provide to others as means of your successful life?

Through this book the author made an attempt in this regard by presenting the essential topics feasible for lecture based presentations as given below.

Chapter 1 introduces the educational system and different types of it along with the importance of value based education for the students. It also provides the major benefits of opting for value based educational system to both students and administration.

Chapter 2 on lighting up the values, provides the list of different qualities (to have a good foundation in their life) that are to be imbibed by the present students.

Chapter 3 on Educational and professional ethics, details the need of ethics in one's life and how these values are the real valuables in our life. It provides the scope of imparting ethics and values in the educational system. Further, it gives the details of positive and negative attitudes of professionals and steps to make work as worship.

Chapter 4 gives the actual meaning and important qualities of true friendship and love. With the help of stories from epics, this chapter provides the discussions regarding true friendship with an example and also mentions the basic difference between love and lust.

Chapter 5 on dealing with habits provides details of different types of habits and how some of them are harmful. It also discusses the causes of addicting to bad habits more easily by the present day young generation and provides the methods for saying a big 'No' to them.

Chapter 6 on how to deal stress mentions the importance of recognizing the most dangerous disease called 'stress' and its causes. It also provides effect of this stress in student life and makes us learn how to deal with this stress factor. Lastly the solutions to the problem of stress were discussed to manage this factor properly.

Chapter 7 on time management furnishes the importance of time and how one should utilize it properly especially during student life. It also gives time management matrix for its effective usage along with wisdom for effective time management.

Chapter 8 on self empowerment provides need for managing one's own self in the present day scenario with the powerful tool of 'working smarter but not harder'. This chapter also informs the self control mechanism to achieve tremendous will power and then how one can stop worrying and start living happily.

Chapter 9 on leadership principles emphasizes the need of good leadership in the present day society along with a good foundation through the qualities of a true leader. With the help of examples of good leaders this chapter encourages all the young student friends who are pursuing their studies to become good leaders in the present day society.

A small topic on Indian culture is also presented in the form of annexure for reading. This chapter provides the valuable wisdom we can learn from the wonderful culture of this great nation. Lastly, it also mentions about the great Indian contribution towards science and engineering. Hence, through different contents of this book an effort is made to extract the essential qualities which will help the young generation to lay a good foundation in making them as good leaders.

Before you begin the first chapter, the author wish to offer sincere thanks to the administration and students of our institute for giving a chance to serve centre for value education, which has given required encouragement for the pursuit of this book. Author also expresses his gratitude to all gurus who have enlightened to present this book for the entire student fraternity.

INTRODUCTION

Education

Life is Education and education is life. Entire humanity spends a lot of their valuable time in learning many new things which are useful for their life (starting from childhood to old age) either directly or indirectly through "Education". Education is the process which involves acquisition, cultivation and dissemination of knowledge. In the entire creation, only humans (the civilized living beings) undergo the task of acquiring knowledge especially through educational procedures. Some of the Holy Scriptures explain that knowledge awakens everyone to the reality of life and is meant to help raise our consciousness from lower to higher levels.

Humans differ from animals only by way of education, which is the technique of transmitting civilization. For humans, either through temples, mosques, churches, family, school or otherwise, there must be a unifying moral code along with some rules for the game of life, and to cultivate some order and regularity along with some direction and stimulus to have a proper civilization. And finally there must be some type of education which acts as a technique, however primitive it may be for the transmission of culture. The culture (topics like its knowledge, its values, morals and manners, its technology and arts along with the language) must be handed down to the younger generations either through imitation or instruction; through parents, or teacher, or priest. This type of tool acts as the very instrument through which they can be transformed from uncivilized to civilized living beings. The disappearance of some of these conditions from any standard system of culture, may destroy a civilization.

Many theorists feel that the entire world has now become integrated into a single civilization of world system, a process known as "globalization". In the entire world, different civilizations and societies all over the globe are economically, politically, and even culturally are interdependent in many ways. The only difference of globalization process of today and that of previous historical ages is that today business markets are the drivers of globalization and in previous ages, it was driven by mutual needs, understanding, healthy exchange of ideas and knowledge. Quality and nature of education could be attributed as the major cause of difference in the globalization process of today and the previous ages.

During previous ages, education used to stress upon the character formation based on spiritual values, and was fostered by a simple and natural lifestyle. Humans were taught to keep their material needs basic, and were trained to meet them by harmonious interaction with nature by following the principle of "simple living and high thinking" - a truly holistic approach to life. The ultimate goal of an education system is not to secure employment or a better position, but to make the younger generation good humans with proper character and life style.

Types of Education

In general the educational system has five components like definition, disposition, delivery of knowledge, design of curriculum and direction or purpose. Inadequacy in application of any one of these components can make that education incomplete. The entire education process in general can be divided into five different categories as given below.

1. **Formal education**: Formal education is a system that has a set of formal curriculum to be studied within a designated period of time, generally at some prescribed location such as a school, college or

university building meant for that purpose. Most modern educational institutions follow a day school formula, where both students and teachers meet for the period of study in the class rooms. Teachers receive a fixed salary and students pay tuition fees for enrolment. Formal education is generally managed by educational institutions which are supported by state or national governments, through their departments of education run by elected ministers of education. The aim of such education will vary depending on political policies established by the current government. These policies generally take into consideration business and industrial needs, and market demand for trained manpower. Formal education incorporates sophisticated schedule of time tables, entrance examinations, mid and end-term tests, a highly competitive spirit of performance, professionally trained and paid educators and staff who teach and administer the affairs of the educational institute.

2. **Non-formal education:** This type of education refers to programs, especially for adults, given at community colleges, through correspondence courses by mail or through long-distance education by internet and the like. Non-formal education would refer to all types of education wherein people take up some kind of apprenticeship or vocational training.

3. **Informal education:** In many ways informal education today and in the past has remained the same. Whatever knowledge one gains, through his daily contact with different persons, by observing oneself or through personal study or by hearing from different sources – all these fall into the category of informal education.

4. **Lifelong education:** This is relatively a new term or ideology for the modern world which has become more popular within the last few decades. The concept of lifelong education is to encourage all individuals to continue the learning process throughout their life time. Learning or education, therefore, is not seen as something one does during one's "school years" only, but rather as an on-going activity.

5. **Value education:** Value education is the system based on purpose of leading the individuals along with entire society towards perfection of life. It takes into account the fullness of human beings in terms of

their physical, emotional, intellectual and social needs in addition to spiritual needs.

Importance of value education

In modern times, at schools and colleges the young generation is learning many things about solids, liquids, gases – their physical and chemical properties, etc. They also study history and geography to know something about past happenings and the structure of the earth. Later students specialize in Science, Commerce, Engineering or Medicine - studying more about body, world and transaction of money, etc. But, no university is able to impart knowledge about the real person of a human being i.e. the soul, and is not putting efforts to answer questions like - Who are you? Why are you suffering? Who is God? How to pray to God? How to perform meditation? How to bring out the innate qualities of the soul like love, peace, serenity, joy, kindness, truthfulness, honesty, character, integrity, etc., and simultaneously give up bad tendencies like greed, pride, lust, anger, etc.

The overall purpose of education is to enable man to live a fulfilling life with a proper goal. Therefore, it is the responsibility of academicians to train students on the issues of character, life style and life goals. In this context, it becomes essential to impart the knowledge of what is really valuable to the present generation. Therefore the subject that deals with this type of knowledge is called "Value Education" and is considered to be very important element in the present educational system.

Necessity of Value based education in the modern society

In general, technology is a conscious application of science and its sole aim is to increase the good of mankind. Technology is the biggest single factor for increased productivity and development. Technology is expected to nurture these urges. But when technology is added to human values it is a boon to the society, whereas, the same technology without human values is a curse to it. Therefore, we need to integrate human values and ethics along with morals in a holistic manner in the present technical education system, to ensure that technology enables growth, prosperity, human development with good quality of life and results finally in happiness.

In modern times, human intelligence has been used primarily to develop material knowledge, especially technology. Technology gratifies our senses, inflates our ego and makes us feel comfortable and proud.

It is a fact that technology provides   entertainment, not peace;
                                          comforts, not happiness;
                                          medicines, not health;
                                          cosmetics, not youth;
                                          life support systems, not life.

Thus technology is like a painkiller that covers, but doesn't cure the pain of our suffering in this material existence. Worse still, it creates an illusory sense of well-being, which makes people feel that the spiritual solution is not necessary. Instead of simple living and high thinking, people are simply living and hardly thinking. Infatuated by promises of a hi-tech paradise, people don't even think about the spiritual purpose of life, erroneously considering it to be unscientific and out dated.

The basic difference between ancient technology and modern technology is that the former helped people to achieve the goal of life, while the latter causes people to forget the goal of life. A question may therefore arise, "Do we have to give up technology and return to village life?" We don't have to give up technology; but we do have to give up the illusion that technology alone can make us happy. We have to adopt the cure of spirituality for attaining real happiness. For example, if we are diseased, we need not avoid taking up the painkiller; but we do have to give up the illusion that the painkiller will cure the disease. But it is only the correct medicine that goes to the root cause of disease and provides relief from it. Therefore, it is the dire necessity in present day modern society to have values, morals and ethics - based educational system. With such an effort, we can impart the most valuable things into minds of present day youth so that they can live with real and true happiness.

Hari Krishna Padavala

Major Benefits of Value Education in Professional Institutes

National Institute of Technology, Warangal is one of the institutes of national importance in technical education under the Ministry of Human Resource Development, Government of India. Formerly known as the Regional Engineering College, Warangal was the first among 17 Regional Engineering Colleges established in India which had the privilege of having the foundation stone being laid by the first prime minister Pandit Jawaharlal Nehru during 1959. The institute awards Bachelor's, Master's and Doctoral degrees in engineering and technology, and master's and doctoral degrees in basic sciences and management. Totally the institute offers eight undergraduate programmes in engineering, thirty post graduate programmes in engineering, sciences and management along with doctoral programs. The institute has about 4500 students residing in the hostels of campus.

In recent times, the author (an alumnus) along with others could notice tangible deviation in the behaviour of students at this institute, in terms of their thinking, life style, habits, relationships, attitude and responsibility besides skills like time and stress management. Therefore, observing the need for imparting value education at the institute, an attempt has been made through the centre for value education to develop suitable type of inputs in imparting values, ethics and morals for achieving the following objectives:

1. To help students appreciate the essential complementary between values and skills for ensuring sustained happiness and prosperity.
2. To facilitate the development of a holistic perspective among students towards life and profession based on correct understanding of the human reality. Such a holistic perspective forms the basis of universal human values and movement towards value based living in a natural way.
3. To highlight the advantages of having Holistic understanding of life in terms of ethical human conduct, trustfulness and mutually fulfilling human behaviour and mutually enriching interaction with nature.

In the background of noticeable success achieved at this institute, the present book provides details about the information related to type of value education principles to be imparted to the present day youth. This book also details about all observed advantages of imparting such a value based education to the students of professional institutes and also to the administration.

Benefits for students

The ten major benefits that are observed from the students who started the process of value education are as follows:

1. Concentrating on Academics

In general, many students work very hard under the guidance of their parents, teachers and mentors till +2 level and for competitive entrance exams to enter good professional institutes. But once they enter into their dream universities / colleges / reputed institutes, they aspire for more freedom and may neglect their academics. Some students by the end of their first year itself, are found to lose interest in academics, as they waste time in things like gossiping, internet browsing, parties and other entertainment procedures. But the students who follow principled life based on values are found to be more responsible towards their academics without wasting their valuable time and in 90% of the cases they could improve their performance in terms of grades quite remarkably.

2. Respecting elders

It's a general observation that some of today's modern youth are not much worried about respecting elders like parents, grandparents and teachers. These relationships are a reality of life for the entire humanity as we are born into these relationships. As modern society started giving importance to material things like money over relationships, younger generation is in great danger by not properly maintaining their relationships which is going to affect them in their life. But, the parents of students who started practicing principled life claim that they are very happy about the behaviour of their children in this aspect. Some parents have enquired the reason for their son's/ daughter's change in life style along with their attitude and with the inspiration of their kids, they themselves have started their new and enriched lives by following some spiritual principles. By this way there are some cases where the entire family got benefited because of one person becoming a principled human being.

3. *To live ourselves with God and nature*

The rules and regulations mentioned in the Holy Scriptures through moral stories are similar to the operating manual that comes with a machine. Through such a manual, we can know what is right and what is wrong; what is good for health and what is bad for health; what will give long-term satisfaction and what is short-term pleasure etc. By following the instructions given in scriptures, one can live happily and those who break the laws should be ready to suffer. One who smokes suffers from lung cancer, one who drinks liquor suffers from liver problem, one who eats junk food gets stomach problem, one who does bad gets bad inevitably. Therefore, by following principled life style, students could clearly demarcate between what is good and what is bad for them. After learning do's and dont's of living, they are able to follow the correct path by avoiding wrong things in relation to nature and God.

4. *To behave in a way that brings happiness to us and others*

A scientist with character, love for God and mankind along with certain values can create something like a life-saving drug while the other invents a bomb that destroys entire cities and cause pain and deformities even to future generations. Atheistic people who do not know the goal of life, bring pain for all other living beings, whereas people with devotion to God have a proper goal for their lives and will always be happy with whatever they have and in turn will try to bring happiness to others also.

5. *To appropriately behave in changing situations of good and bad times that we are put in*

Beauty, good education, high birth, wealth – all can make one too proud and lead one to act in ways that will harm those who possess them. Cultivating values teach us that these opulence's are gifts of God awarded to us in this life, but they are all temporary and will pass away with time. Thus learning values makes one sober and cool headed. As all of us know, it is a fact that life is always not a bed of roses - many people who own multinational companies flourished in luxurious facilities but when they faced sudden problems in life, some of them lost all the money and committed suicide. Value education teaches us how to be courageous and composed in the face of problems and how to tackle different situations of life.

6. *To lay a foundation of habits and character that brings peace and happiness*

The education received in school or college can be compared to a beautiful house. Value education is the foundation on which this house is built. If foundation is strong and sturdy, house will stand well for long time to come. Somebody may say, "We need only a beautiful house and what is the need of foundation which is underground that consumes time and money." But such a person is certainly foolish; because he does not know that without foundation the whole skyscraper will collapse. Similarly, without investing our time in cultivating the foundation of character and habits, no one can expect to become peaceful or happy in life. Because of value educational programs at our institute, some of the students could study Holy Scriptures and could inculcate good habits and very importantly good character which makes them always peaceful and happy.

7. *To recognize how Eastern culture is glorious for Vedic heritage*

In early 1990s, American government began to study why Japanese business was more successful than American business, even though Americans had better schools and more facilities. The researchers discovered that success is more related to the Japanese mentality than American technology. The Japanese companies were built on values like team effort and relationship etc. and any management success depend on technique and values. Management research shows that we may get the hand and head of a person to work but we can get the heart of the person only when he has a life of values. Therefore, cultures with very deep spiritual roots have competitive advantage which is now being realized by present day management experts who are trying to find some solutions to the organizational problems from Indian culture and its spiritual wisdom. By knowing the Vedic heritage of India, students started appreciating their country and are trying to do their best to make this country glorious in the days to come.

8. *To learn Self discipline*

What would happen in a garden if every plant grew as it liked without being trimmed? There would be no beauty. Similarly in school student must become a plant to be moulded by the teachers through discipline in order to achieve true success. A person without self discipline or control allows his senses to go astray according to their demands. The result is that one suffers from greed, anger, envy, laziness, overeating, pride etc. Whereas, students with controlled mind could manage alluring sensual disturbances with their intelligence to discriminate good and bad things and could make situations advantageous in their lives.

9. *To become Responsible*

Can a student always do what he likes? Say, for example can he play cricket all the day and miss the school or college? Or can he watch television or internet all the time, ignoring his exam the next day. Such activities indicate the students' irresponsibility towards duties. Value education teaches how to be cheerful, tolerant, enthusiastic and simultaneously be responsible in fulfilling one's duties. By reading the biographies of great personalities like Gandhi, Socrates, Einstein etc. who are responsible for their work, one can understand that they all great souls who lived by values and achieved glory in life. Hence, after understanding their greatness, some students are able to use their precious time in moulding their lives the best possible way.

10. *To be Loved by all*

If you are cheerful, people feel good being with you. If you are honest, sincere, respectful and affectionate others would love to become your friend. Nobody likes a cheater or an arrogant person. Value education helps you to acquire these qualities without difficulty. One who lives by values and not by dishonesty, manipulation etc. has nothing to fear in this world. When you talk sweetly on the face of a person and badmouth him on his back, then your conscience will keep troubling you. But one who lives by pure values of honest and respectful behaviour will never behave duplicitously. As the students who started practicing principled life were pious and were not indulging in any of the malpractices like ragging etc the fellow student community and the faculty members could appreciate them. Hence, these students besides possessing peace of mind within them are being loved by all those around them.

Benefits for administration

In any college or university, if we can bring a change in the behavior of student community along with the added benefits as mentioned above, the college administration can find the following changes in their campus.

1. Students becoming well mannered and grateful to the school/ college/university.
2. Proper ambience in campus, without any clashes amongst the student community.
3. Reduction in ragging menace.
4. Proper culture of good friendship among students.
5. Students become respectful and appreciative of all the cultural festivals.
6. Reduction of suicide attempts by students.
7. Dedicated faculty - as they feel more commitment to their duty.
8. Good teacher – student relationship.
9. Proper knowledge transfer because of educational and professional ethics.
10. Increase in the overall recognition of the school/college/university because of good feedback from students, parents and also from organizations coming for placements.

Hence, people in the administration can be more peaceful in organizing / managing the affairs of the school/college/university.

Aims of the book

Present book is aimed at addressing following important points that are necessary in the present day student life, so that he will not face any major problem in his academics, professional, family and also in personal life.

1. To familiarize the students with the key concepts like importance of morals, values and ethics.
2. To help students in identifying and resisting unethical behaviour.
3. To provide direction to the students on how to introduce such an ideology of having value based life both individually and collectively for the benefit of the society.
4. To teach theoretical as well as practical aspects of the ancient Vedic aphorism of "life is education and education is life".
5. To bring solutions to many of our present day individual and social anomalies, within the context of our modern education.
6. To bring peace and harmony along with real happiness in to the lives of modern young generation, who are basic pillars of tomorrow's society.

Necessity of the book

As a faculty member and being in-charge of the Center for Value Education of our prestigious institute, I have been working in the direction of imparting values into the lives of our young students. The general secretary of center for value education and the president of the student's council for academic year 2012-2013 used to interact with me over different issues related to the student community along with learning how to improve their skills for a better life style. For the benefit of student community, they have requested me to provide information about **"the importance and methods of adding values to life"** preferably in the form of a book.

For this purpose, a survey was conducted through members of our center to get feedback on the problems faced by student community.

From this feedback, the required areas where students are facing troubles were identified and efforts were made to give some simple yet effective solutions based on principles from Holy Scriptures.

The present day student community is deviating from the actual purpose or true goals of human life. Many times, students are not clear in their understanding of basic necessities of life and are unable to adopt the right way to reach true happiness and love. Simultaneously, they were not properly guided in having answers to questions like what is really important in life? What is true success and what are the things that are truly required for humans? How a human being is intelligent and different from other living entities? Modern educational system in general and society along with family in particular, are unable to guide the young generation in getting correct answers to such questions. Therefore a need is felt to guide students in getting knowledge of leading a value based life. This book is mainly aimed at answering such types of valuable questions with value based information. If a student understands and follows these principles, he will certainly discover the right path to the goal of human life.

Theme of the book: "Adding values to life"

Being in one of the Eastern cultured countries like India, people are unable to understand the glorious culture as well as the eminent personalities who lived here with great character. Eastern culture is not based on putting lifelong efforts for endeavoring to get more wealth, gorgeous homes, fast foods and horrible entertainment methods. It is based on rich Vedic knowledge, which actually aims at something higher. This culture makes humans understand basic purpose of life along with its true goal. It also aims at nurturing people in society to develop great competence, good character and proper behavior.

In addition, India had a great legendary culture starting from Harappa. The long period of invasions by different people of different origin and life style, along with their efforts at breaking the culture made lot of changes in the Indian society. This country produced personalities like Mahatma Gandhi who got us independence based on the principle of non-violence.

Eastern culture is based on the strength of values with which the people lived in the mode of goodness especially in India. Values teach people what is good or bad and simultaneously what is important or useless. Therefore, through this book an attempt is made to provide information regarding the importance of adding values to life and thereby equipping the younger generation in having happy and peaceful lives.

LIGHTING UP VALUES

For any human being, happiness and prosperity are the universal aspirations. Many times, all humans are tirelessly working for fulfilment of these basic aspirations in accordance with their personal understanding or perception on what is happiness and prosperity. To seek is the nature of any living force that is present in all human beings and the search seems never ending. The real need in the present day modern scenario is not just to seek, but to seek from the right source. The best source that is available for all human beings is education and through this educational process one can primarily develop the right understanding about human life. Needless to say, the success of any educational system depends on the extent to which it can guide the humanity for achieving the basic aspirations of human beings.

In the present day educational system, students after completing their education are generally found to be indulging in indecisive decisions and sometimes fail in their attempts to reach their goals. Finally, students are unable to contribute any tangible thing to society as they could not feel the true happiness and prosperity in their lives. This is because of the reason that most of the students are thinking the advanced science and technology that prevails today will give happiness and peace in their lives. However, it is a fact that the use of science and technology can only contribute to human welfare provided it should be associated with proper wisdom and values in their lives.

Modern educational procedure provides the required skills and techniques to earn money without emphasising the value dimension in student's lives. Young generation should be taught about what is valuable and what is really valuable in their lives, which is being dealt through value education program. Values are the principles or qualities humans should possess which can make them useful to the society along with providing real happiness and prosperity in their lives.

Values based life

Values based life means creating the in-built mechanism which distinguishes right from wrong. In addition, it also imparts do's and don'ts of our actions. It also acts as the basis of choosing between alternative courses of action when a critical decision needs to be taken in life. In general, value based life style lead to fair and objective decisions along with actions so that the welfare of all the people is ensured. But low values based life does exactly the opposite which may lead to havoc in the humanity. These facts can be extended to all facets of our life - personal, family, professional and spiritual. When anyone lives with high values, he embodies all the necessary qualities of a good human being.

Present Day Materialistic Approach

In 21st century, the materialism has started for exploiting men, materials and nature in the name of making human life more comfortable. Many times, people search for their so called comfortable zone with the "more to achieve" syndrome. To achieve such a comfortable zone sometimes people have to face cut throat competition, start exploiting other living beings in addition to the nature itself. The so called comfortable zone which is based on the economical growth aspect will result in degradation of morals, principles of philosophy, following the culture etc. And because of degradation of positive aspects along with negative impact of many advanced facilities like internet and communication system resulted in considerable behavioural changes in the present day student community. Because of the imbalance between the valuable values inherited from our past lives and the present day technically advanced lifestyle, people start opting for the short lived or temporary happiness principles based on the wealth concept without having any inclination for the eternal or real happiness in their lives.

Importance of values in human lives

Humans, who are considered to be the most intelligent living beings on this universe are thinking in the direction of attaining the real happiness. In the present day society, economical based lifestyle is causing frustration to humanity which can be curtailed only through spiritual philosophy. Philosophy of any kind will try to impart love of wisdom or knowledge. When the sun shines on a snow-capped mountain, the layers of snow melt down helplessly. Similarly, when the sun like wisdom or knowledge shines on any living entity, layers of ignorance start melting away, thus uncovering the inner soul enlightenment.

Mark Twain observed even decades ago that "In religion, India is the only millionaire". In the present day life, we are witnessing an extraordinary worldwide spiritual renaissance. Interestingly, the global interest in Indian spirituality has inspired many thoughtful Indians to re-examine their own cultural legacy. Our ancient Indian culture used to be spiritual based one providing proper balance between science and religion with out driving the human life for the only material welfare zone. The general life style of any human being used to possess three dimensions like physical, psychological and importantly spiritual which could provide the society with virtuous behaviour and positive values. These values can be broadly classified into five categories of self oriented, family oriented, nature oriented, society oriented and spiritual oriented ones (figure). Although there are different headings of values, let us make an effort to light up some basic values that were coming from the ancient eastern culture and it is sure that if they are inculcated into our lives, these values will make the humans more useful to the society.

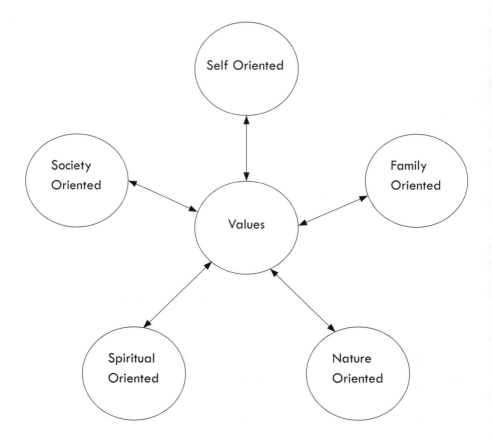

Wisdom tree

Wisdom is the quality of having experience, knowledge and good judgement about the truths of life. The type of knowledge that not only just provides information but also transforms a person is called as wisdom literature. Wisdom is the art of converting an experience into learning. Every experience one undergoes in the course of life is like a seed and the learning that comes from that experience is like a tree. As we know big trees also manifest from a tiny /small seeds. People out of ignorance may misjudge the depth of content that is stored in the tiny seed.

From every aspect of the tree one can taste a different flavour of wisdom. If we consider the stem of a tree, it has so many layers, each layer indicating one experience in its life. Just like each layer will add strength to the tree, every experience add another layer of strength to our life. Needless to say, a tree is generally judged by its quality in fruits. A caring gardener will wait patiently for the tree to manifest its sweet fruits. But in reality there may be some bitter fruits also which may be manifesting from the same tree and these bitter fruits also teaches us many lessons. In our life, if we attempt to seek only sweet fruits similar to happiness, then we may land up in unexpected annoyance after having bitter ones similar to sorrow moments of life. Therefore, it is necessary some times to learn something sweet that is lying even with in the bitter fruit also which makes the person to be matured in his life.

Good foundation to excel in life

The type of foundation (which may not be seen by any one) decides functioning or performance of a building. Similarly, agood foundation interms of proper values, ethics and morals will make a person to excel in his life. The foundation of a tree is not above the ground, but it is within the ground in the form of roots. If our life is based on sound principles similar to that of a good foundation, no matter how many setbacks comes in our life, these principles will help us to tolerate them easily.

In nature, the Sun gives light and this type of illumination signifies for knowledge and freedom from the ignorance and darkness. This torchlight of knowledge which may be derived from the Holy Scriptures like Bhagavad-Gita, Ramayanam, Srimad Bhagavatam, Bible or Quran will dissipate the darkness of our ignorance. In the case of a tree, the leaf traps the energy of the sun and combines it with water from its root along with some carbon dioxide from the atmosphere to nourish the entire tree. Similar to the leaf of a tree, we can also make an effort to lighten up ourselves though the energy of the sun by learning the basic values with which we can live happily.

Compassion

The fundamental craving from all living entities (including humans) is for experiencing the pleasure. This principle is same from the lowest of insects to the great kings and presidents. Everyone is seeking for pleasure, but there is only one pleasure that can reach the important part of our body (i.e. heart) — need to love someone and simultaneously receive it back. Generally, people may strive for acquiring wealth and hanker for sensual pleasures along with fame which may reach the mind and senses only. These types of pleasures don't really touch the heart of the person. Just for an example, can one be happy if he is the only person on the entire earth and is the sole proprietor of everything on the earth. Certainly not because there will be no one to love and there will be no one to be loved by you. The nature of living entities is - they need love at all times.

Practically speaking, the common thing in every spiritual path is the characteristic of compassion. In general, one who follows the spiritual path is an instrument of compassion. For example, Lord Buddha taught about ahimsa, means non-violence, respecting the integrity of life of all living beings and to be compassionate towards others. Similarly, in Jain religion, they follow strict vegetarianism because they want to reduce the amount of violence by killing some other living creatures. In muslim community, they will be totally fasting entire day during Ramzan month to develop the attitude of compassion — one of my good friends told me that during fasting they will understand the pains of hunger and so they will greatly feel compassionate for any person who is suffering from hunger and they will be readily helping such type of people. Hence, the highest and most pleasing service that one can offer is to accept inconvenience and difficulty in order to show care and compassion for others.

Love gives but greed takes

The education we had and the knowledge we acquired should never be used to simply fulfill our greed to earn more. If people use knowledge and education to satisfy their greed, the society will end in a big havoc. By nature our consciousness is for full of joy and there can be no chance for any greed. The real joy and love wants only to be shared with everyone else. And it is fact that the nature of love is to give; whereas the nature of greed is to take.

From the day we took birth, we feel the real joy and pleasure in giving love of our hearts to others. During childhood people will not be selfish and will be sharing love and joy with as many people they come across. But once they grew up their consciousness gets impure and people develop the selfish attitude and rather than giving some thing to others they wish to take anything and everything from others. This can be avoided with the help of purification process of our hearts which will make our consciousness clear and transparent just like a mirror gets clarity by dusting it off. And this purification process for the heart is possible by remembering God at every moment. One may call God with different names like Allah, Jehovah, Buddha, Rama or Krishna, but actually there is only one Supreme God, who is the object of love and source of all that exists.

Perfect charity

Charity is generally known to be the activity for donating or serving liberally for the benefit of the poor or needy in relieving their distress. To give charity for getting the name and fame is also good but it doesn't touch the heart of anyone. But if one gives charity because you actually feel for the suffering of some one else and out of love you really want to help that person that is real charity.

Charity is of three types: charity for the body, charity for the mind and charity for the soul. To give food, shelter and clothes is charity for the body while the act of encouraging people to be good to others and to be friendly is charity of the mind. To give transcendental knowledge and facilities for people to be educated in spiritual life is charity for the soul. All these three types should go together side by side. One should be good, charitable and pious but at the same time one should also know what is the best charity for the human beings. For example, if one can feed a hungry man, it is a good thing, but after some time, he becomes hungry again. If you can teach that person about spiritual aspects of life and develop devotional consciousness, he will never come to you with hunger problem any more because that person has achieved a step ahead of his body consciousness. So therefore, the activity of giving spiritual knowledge is the perfect charity. And with such knowledge, there is enlightenment in the hearts of people through which one can utilize human form of life for the greatest benefit.

From spiritual point of view, the rich people are found to be more poverty stricken than poor people in terms of peace and happiness. We all should definitely help the poor by giving what they want to maintain their bodies, health and other physical needs and at the same time we should not neglect the rich people also interms of providing peace and happiness to them. It's not a surprising fact that about 80% of people in the higher income group are taking to artificial methods like sleeping pills to go to bed, which is actually a natural phenomenon for the remaining people. What does that mean? They may have many things like big bungalow, wonderful cars, comfortable water beds, silken clothes, all kinds of workers and security devices with them, but still they can not get sleep as they are more affected with anxiety. Whereas, some people who are in less income or average income group will immediately go to sleep with in no time, because of peace of mind they have. Therefore, all sectors of the society are in need of charity in one or the other way and universally they are in need of charity for the transcendental knowledge.

Contentment

In the present day technically advanced world, most of the people are suffering from the discontent disease, due to which they are unable to have peace of mind. The scientists, engineers and technologists are thinking that by creating luxurious type of lifestyle, people will become content. But, many times people have the required facilities and luxuries for proper functioning of their life, still they hanker for newer and newer things.

It's really a difficult task to find any one who can say that "Yes, I am very happy with what ever I have". Occasionally, we may find someone in that way of happiness for some period of time, but if we examine him the next time when he loses those things will lament and comes in to the zone of unhappiness. As the nature of the world is to have changes continuously, things in and around us are also liable to change. Our human life is meant for the ultimate pleasure along with some contentment. If one is having contentment attitude with what ever minimum things he has or exhibit for a smooth life, then naturally he will be the happiest person in the world. And this will only be possible by having ultimate realization of the love of God and without such realization, a human will be miserable, unfortunate and discontent.

Humility

Humility means being honest and truthful. One can think of oneself for what do we have done such a great thing to feel proud of ourselves. If God does not make the sun rise, what can a person do? In similar grounds, if we think of the person who has created different parts of our body like brain, eyes, tongue, stomach, heart, intestines and others? If one analyses his body interms of shape, parts and their arrangement one can surely appreciate its design by the supreme designer God. As the people in British Parlance say, "Do not be proud of borrowed plumes" – meaning that whatever we exhibit is not actually ours, it was given by the God. And we have the free will to use what God gives us either in a good way or in a bad way or also in a spiritual way.

As the living beings, God has given such a free will for all of us and according to the free will what we do and what we say, the karma is going to come back on us. One may be strong in young age but by the power of time how long one can remain strong and young. This uncontrollable and unstoppable time factor makes the strongest person also to be the weakest person. For example, popular boxing champion like Mohammad Ali, who is considered to be the greatest among all the men few decades ago, is now suffering from Parkinson disease because of which he can not lift his own cup of coffee. Therefore all of us both in terms of body and mind are under the control of nature. So humility means knowing what we are honestly.

To achieve any thing good in this world is difficult and some times it is like a struggle in life. For example, a bird in order to fly in the air has to beat its wings continuously. Similarly, a swimmer has to continuously beat his hands and legs in order to swim in water. Needless to mention, the moment the bird stops beating its wings, it begins to fall. And similarly the moment swimmer stops beating his legs, he begins to drown. Therefore to maintain anything we have to struggle in one way or other.

In this world, generally everyone wants honour and respect. It is the nature of illusion to pull our consciousness down to the egoistic platform but being the most intelligent creatures of this world, we have to struggle against the tendency of egoism and exploitation. We should take the position of being humble — not to exploit others but to serve them in a proper way; not to seek respect from everyone but to give respect to all.

Love means to give and by giving we receive the same

In nature, the essential need within every living entity is to seek for pleasure in their activities. For example, an ant attains its pleasure by getting a grain of sugar and a moth will attain its pleasure in approaching to light. And we all have observed what type of struggle they do even at the risk of their lives to attain that grain of sugar or to achieve that light. For some kind of people, their pleasure is to satisfy their ego by causing pain and harm to others. And some others find their pleasure in being famous, adored, worshipped and aggrandized. Now-a-days most of the humanity is running to find pleasure by the acquisition of wealth, property and the power which comes with all these things.

Everyone is looking for pleasure in this world. That essential need for pleasure, in its most important form, is the pleasure of love. Even if you were the proprietor of entire property on the earth but if you are alone then you can never be happy. There can be no real satisfaction for the heart without having people to love and being loved by others. Therefore, the real problem in the world is poverty of the heart and the only way to fill that hunger is love as this is the only thing that touches our heart.

To love means to give. For example, mother finds pleasure in giving satisfaction to her child and similarly father finds pleasure in seeing the family prospering nicely. The child as such gives nothing to parents, but they find more happiness in serving that child rather than anything else. So this is the real pleasure, love is not just to take but to give. The more you give and the more genuine your giving is, the more people will naturally reciprocate, thus bringing satisfaction to the heart.

On the other hand, if you do not feel loved by others, it is probably because you are not showing love properly. And similarly, if you do not feel respected, it is probably because you are not showing respect to others in a correct way. In general, the human nature is that people reciprocate with what you give them. If you do not show care and affection for others, people will probably ignore you and that is the human nature. If you insult others, you draw their anger and if you praise others you draw their praise. And similarly, if you are affectionate to others, you can draw out whatever affection is within their hearts. Therefore, in giving we receive anything in this nature.

Attitude

In nature, the way we react to opportunities that come in our life depends a lot on our attitude. In fact the entire world is nothing but our vision covered by our attitude. To understand about the right attitude of a person let us make an example from the great epic of Mahabharata. Dronacharya who is the teacher of both Pandavas and Kauravas once asked his student Yudhisthira to go into the world in search of a person who was worse than himself. And similarly he also asked Duryodhana to find some one who was better than him. Yudhisthira came back and reported that he could not find any one worse than him and he also said that everyone he met has some good quality which he himself did not possess. It means that his constant observation was of his own personal defects and others' good qualities. On the other hand, Duryodhana came back and claimed that he could not find any one better than him and he said that he has found atleast one defect in everyone that he himself did not possess.

Here we have to understand that both were the students of the same teacher Dronachaya and they have learned so many things from that great teacher. But there is lot of difference in their way of seeing the world because of the difference in their frames of mind. Their attitude, which was controlled by the culture in which they were raised, the kind of influence they had around themselves and the inner desires they nurtured could influence their way of concluding differently for the similar kind of situation. Therefore, it is important for all of us to have proper attitude along with the vision for entire world around us. If we make friendship with those who has good qualities and behaviour along with right attitude then naturally we also can develop those good qualities in our lives.

Learning how to be successful even from Failures

One famous speaker said "Success is nothing but going from failure to failure, without losing one's enthusiasm". We really never fail until we give up trying – trying with determination and enthusiasm. And vision in life means to see the invisible, to feel the intangible and to achieve the impossible.

For example, Thomas Edison tried 8000 times various experiments before he finally invented the electric bulb. Later when he was asked by media people and others about his 8000 failures, he said that he was not discouraged by all these 8000 failures. Rather he expressed that from every failure, he learned that what doesn't work for electrical bulb. That type of attitude made him to succeed in his effort of trying again and again without losing the enthusiasm.

Actually, the challenges or failures can either be stepping stones or stumbling blocks on the road of success for any person. It is all a matter of how we look at them. We can see a glass of water either as half-full or we can see the same glass as half-empty. One way of seeing will bring us enthusiasm, while the other way of seeing will bring us discouragement. We can learn some thing even from a mistake; a mistake will remain as mistake if we fail to learn from it. Real and great leaders will make many, many mistakes but they do not repeat them. They learn from that mistake and being determined along with remaining enthusiasm they will reach the goal. In any situation, the actual champions are always focussed on their main goals.

It is not a surprising thing that the failures build proper character also. Failure is something that only comes to one who earns it. One should learn the art of respecting the failure as honour. We can not be successful unless we have the courage to fail. And every failure contains the seed of success. By learning from our mistakes and failures, we become stronger and stronger and we develop greater integrity in our life. When difficulties, obstacles and failures trouble our lives, we should always be courageous seeing the invisible and simultaneously feeling the intangible. And if we follow this way, we can surely achieve the impossible things also in our life. One may not understand the exact cause behind the difficulty, but if we have faith, if we have hope, we can always be looking for that flower that will grow from the rainstorm. That type of attitude is the substance of a successful man.

The Scriptures like Bible says the opportunity knocks everyone, but most people complain about the noise. We should see an opportunity in every situation; we never lose the enthusiasm until we stop trying. A third class man does not even begin to endeavour to come out of darkness, because he is fearful that he may fail at any moment. A second class man endeavors, but turns back when faced with obstacles and failures in his path. But the true first class man keeps his mind fixed on the goal with great determination and does not turn back till he achieves that goal.

Of course, through such an endeavour of imparting values into the lives of present day modern youth, we may be hoping to create islands of integrity amidst the swamp of corruption and dishonesty. This type of effort surely requires highest level of dedication from administrators, educators, faculty and importantly from the students. But such a task which may be a difficult one will result in giving right direction to all the professional students to excel in their studies, profession, family, society and more importantly for themselves in the long run of their lives. Therefore, let all of us make a try to imbibe these values to bring unity in the society, nation and world at large.

ETHICS

All over the world, human society is experiencing a great escalation in terms of science & technology. In addition, there is a high jump in the level of knowledge and opportunities to improve the quality of human life. The modern era of high knowledge based society coupled with innovative technology had a great impact on the behaviour of people both at educational institutions and also at work place. The internet facility along with media provides the latest and vast information from all over the globe within a very short time. People can commute very fastly by using automobiles and aeroplanes. Similarly they can communicate with friends and others easily through e-mails and mobiles.

Both men and women who have proper competence and standard calibre can excel in their education along with profession. Sometimes, people with high educational profile and a good job are found to be failing in terms of possessing proper behaviour in their life. Anyone with a strong foundation in terms of values, morals and ethics can be expected to behave properly in life, whereas people devoid of strong moral and ethical foundation can cause sufferings to others in the society by their actions. Therefore, there is a great need in the human society to produce people having strong foundation in terms of values, morals and ethics, which is possible only with introduction of spirituality in them.

Ethics

Ethics are set of principles or morals with a sense of purpose that are required for the civilization of any society. Starting from the dawn of civilization, ethics are followed at different levels which had a great influence of culture, religion along with spiritual wisdom. For the distinction between right and wrong things in life, developing righteous thoughts and actions, living in the mode of goodness and doing good for the benefit of humanity, it is necessary to follow these ethics to the maximum extent possible.

These ethics are generally relative and not absolute ones and some of them in terms of code of conduct have become universal and also fundamental ones for the humanity. We can classify ethics broadly into five categories depending on the level at which people are following them.

1. Personal ethics – based on individuals belief for a better life style
2. Interpersonal ethics – developed for group of individuals
3. Social ethics – developed between different groups/ religions/ cultures etc.
4. Educational ethics – developed for properly educating the new generation
5. Professional ethics – based on the correct practice of profession.

For the sake of young leaders, let us discuss the topics of educational and professional ethics in detail.

Need of ethics

In order to have proper value based life style along with a good code of conduct at every stage of our life; these ethics are essential and have to be introduced into the educational system. Any professional (may be a doctor, scientist, engineer, musician etc) is expected to use his skills and talents for the progress and prosperity of humanity, but not for self aggrandizement. Professionals interface with society at various stages may be as a teacher, professional worker, as a manager or as an owner of an organisation. Therefore, it becomes important to follow ethics and at the same time teach some of them to future generation.

Today, with rapidly spreading globalisation it becomes necessary to follow internationally accepted ethical values along with code of conduct. It therefore, becomes essential for educational institutions and organisations to develop a mind set for the younger generations during their education itself to cultivate a sense of social responsibility so as to uphold the honour and dignity of their profession.

Educational Ethics

In the present educational system, education at college / university is for building a strong foundation for appropriate understanding of the world in terms of science, technology. There is no doubt that such education will produce people of high competence and calibre, so that they can contribute to the progress of human society. But at the same time, we have to agree that today's education is devoid of values, morals and ethics. Hence, today's educational system is unable to create a society with good human values like honesty, truthfulness, non-violence, dignity of labour and unity in diversity. This inability has resulted in increase of social evils with a decrease in the standards of character and conduct due to which violence, terrorism and unrest are causing lot of disturbance in the community. In today's condition, human society in general and young generation in particular, is neglecting the environment around us. For example polluting water, air, uncontrolled deforestation, rise in the levels of greed and lust have become common characteristics.

Some of the observations about present day society are:

(i)   Qualities like selfless service and self sacrifice which were very prominent in our culture earlier are seldom observed, while selfishness and greed have taken over the previous ones. The desire to enrich oneself at the cost of exploiting others has become common in professions and occupations. Now-a-days ethics and morality have declined to the lowest levels and offenses have increased to the highest levels.

(ii)   Rendering hard work to achieve the goal is fading very fast, and at the same time people are opting for easy means to achieve anything. Many times students are opting for short cut methods to get marks in the examinations and then degrees. Sometimes, there is loss of research integrity because of plagiarism even in the best institutes. Any student who indulges in malpractices during education stage can not be honest in professional, family or social life.

(iii)   Caste, community and the linguistic feelings are increasing a lot and thereby resulting in animosity among the people. This type of attitude is posing a serious threat to the cordial relationships in the society.

(iv)   Previously young people used to respect elders and women. But, even this basic quality is eroding very fast in the society although people possess high educational qualifications. Today, women are looked as instruments for enjoyment – this attitude does not speak of high moral character. As a result, now-a-days there is a tremendous increase in atrocities and violence on women.

(v)   More alarmingly, the levels of corruption and misappropriation of public funds have increased a lot in the society. In the name of providing facilities to public, lot of money was misappropriated in many scams in the recent past. Sometimes, members of parliament or assembly, ministers along with administrative officers, in collusion with contractors and mafia leaders are involved in these scams.

(vi)   Surprisingly, sports also have become the place for cheating people at large. Players and organisers of these events are indulging in malpractices to earn easy money.

From the above observations one can conclude that bad and evil forces are taking over the good and vitals of our society. Therefore, there is a dire necessity of an educational system that will ensure a good society as well as prosperity and happiness to the individuals. In such a society, people should be able to create and maintain harmony among themselves and nature.

Missing thing in the present modern educational system

During olden days, education did not mean just acquiring skills for earning. It was focussed on imparting that knowledge which enabled the student to know the nature of internal enemies like lust, greed, anger and pride. And value education used to train students to fight and conquer these enemies. Conquering these enemies does not mean leading a dry life without any desire or ambition? Rather, value education enabled the students to use their intelligence positively in pursuance of enlightenment by connecting with God.

In the modern day society, education mainly focuses on acquiring technical knowledge for earning adequate money for ensuring a comfortable life. This kind of knowledge will neither lead to the development of intellect (ability to recollect and manipulate the so called information) nor the development of intelligence (ability to discriminate between right and wrong). Those educated in this direction are able to control the society around them with material technology but are failing miserably in controlling enemies of the heart or the world within as they have no spiritual knowledge.

Healing the wounded modern world

Qualities like lust, anger, greed and pride are like diseases afflicting the minds of people from their child hood. And by the time they reach their professional or college education these tendencies increase much and take them away from their actual goal of having proper education. The other problems that are observed in today's modern society like disrespecting elders, addiction to drugs, involvement in activities of violence, creating pollution in society are the symptoms of these diseases.

Diagnosing and dealing with such type of diseases is the greatest need that is felt by many intellectuals. People may not be successful in solving these problems through social service. As long as society is unable to realize the great potency of spiritual power to resist and conquer these types of elements, people will become slaves to them. Therefore, the educational system should try to provide education associated with culture and devotion based on the Vedic texts in an appropriate and suitable manner for the present young generation.

The values we have are the real valuables

One has to realize that happiness of human beings depends not on the type of valuables, but on the type of values we have. It is because of this fact that the values we have will shape how we use our valuables and which decides our happiness.

In case our values are materialistic, then we will use our valuables to enjoy for our own selfish satisfaction and for accumulating more material possessions. And materialistic values do not address the actual need of our heart i.e. love. We long to love and expect to be loved. The materialistic values force us to direct our love towards others at the material level only. At the later stage, that type of love can be disrupted or devastated at any moment by the worldly ups and downs.

Holy scriptures indicate that the love which does not have a real and fruitful purpose cannot give real happiness and can neither relieve us from the resulting agony. That's why scriptures recommend changing our values from material to spiritual and directing our true love towards God. If one realizes that the spiritual values we have are the real valuables and should be preserved the same way as we treasure our material valuables, then one can feel true happiness in one's life.

Values to be taught for the present generation

Though there are many valuable values that should be taught to the present modern youth, here is the list of some of the important ones which have been selected based on the fundamental principle of 'Dharma'. As per scriptures, Dharma is not religion but it represents an activity or a process which cannot be changed. For example, liquidity cannot be taken away from water and heat cannot be wiped away from fire. Similarly, the eternal function of any living entity including humans cannot be taken away from the living entity. All the rules of righteous conduct of human beings from time immemorial come under the meaning of this word Dharma. Therefore, based on this principle of dharma, here are the some of the important values that are to be imparted to the present day student community:

1. Our actual duty towards nature and living entities
2. Recognizing the importance of God in our lives
3. Developing selfless service attitude toward God and other living entities
4. Code of conduct for human beings
5. Respect towards elders, guru and women
6. Equanimity towards all
7. Compassion towards others
8. Sacrificing attitude
9. Control over mind and senses
10. Gratitude

Imparting ethics and values during the educational age

As discussed earlier, education does not mean only getting the necessary skills and knowledge to get a job but it also should be able to develop the students' personality by acquiring the desirable qualities like proper behaviour and character. What ever methods we follow to get wealth without putting efforts to have proper character will go waste and by having proper behaviour and character one can live happily with good health even if one has little wealth.

Hence, at the educational level, students should be imparted the two important fundamentals of education. First, to have the necessary knowledge and information along with the desirable tools and skills to get the degree and earn a livelihood which is essential. In addition, every student should also get trained in developing good qualities and love towards others along with love to the supreme Lord.

Integrating spirituality with education

In general, the word spirituality has been misunderstood by many people especially the youth. Spirituality means developing a mindset which is tuned to a higher objective of human existence. The basic objectives include discovering the purpose of life and equipping the person with a bent of mind to serve God, nature and society with devotion and sincerity. Spirituality helps man in establishing harmony with nature and thus invokes one's commitment in preserving the environment. With the integration of spirituality in education, it will ensure that along with getting knowledge through science and technology, people imbibe the necessary values, ethics and morals. Then the students will be able to utilise their education for the good of the society and environment.

Professional Ethics

Any profession, whether it is medical, engineering, administration, management, corporate or public governance in its true sense offers a privilege to the person for rendering service to society. This privilege includes responsibility and commitment for protecting the dignity and maintaining honour of profession. It also necessitates continuous upgradation of knowledge and skills of the person for excelling in the chosen field. Importantly, professional practicing requires high ethical and moral foundation and also honesty, impartiality, truthfulness along with trust worthiness. It also demands that the professional adhere to the governing codes of practice along with moral and ethical values.

In recent years, professional ethics have become very important. As professionals, people are facing complex controversial issues which are hard to digest. Many a times, professional bodies themselves are discussing and developing the necessary guidance for provisions on professional ethics and conduct. These professional ethics help professionals to choose the correct decision when they encounter moral issues.

Hari Krishna Padavala

Positive and Negative attitudes of the professionals

Any activity of a professional in an organisation, can be rendered with a positive attitude or a negative attitude. If the positive ones are more than the negative ones, then there won't be any problem in the smooth running of the organisational set-up. But if the negative factors dominate the positive ones then surely there will be lot of problems in the organisation. Let us now list the types of positive and negative attitudes of the professionals that are generally observed in the modern society.

The general desirable positive attitudes that ought to be observed in any organisation are: dedication, cooperation, team work, compassion, sacrifice, honesty, loyalty, gratitude and hard work along with broad mindedness. Whereas, the negative attitudes that are generally observed are: greed, jealousy, lack of commitment, dishonesty, disinterestedness, discouragement, disloyalty, hatred, back-biting, frustration etc. All these negative attitudes result in lack of cooperation and team work which affects the basic functioning of the organisation.

Some times, the same official may surprisingly be exhibiting both these positive and negative attitudes depending on time, place and circumstances. The behaviour of person may change depending on with whom he is interacting in a particular situation. Some people may be dissatisfied because of a new rule or decision implemented, whereas others may take it in a positive way for the benefit of organisation or society. Hence, we should inculcate positive attitudes and then enact corresponding positive actions to ensure ever lasing peace and happiness at our work places.

The attitude one has either positive or negative, depends on factors like family circumstances during one's childhood which influences the mind in a certain way. These attitudes develop during childhood because of education, family members' behaviour and social conditions. It also depends on the development of personality during secondary and college education period. Ofcourse, even the circumstances during adulthood also influence one's professional behaviour, but predominantly the values and ethics which have been imbibed during youth will have lot of effect on the behaviour as an employee.

If we analyze the entire range of negative attitudes of professionals, one realizes that people have wrongly accepted that happiness and success lie in material possessions and power. From such a materialistic notion all negative attitudes develop and lead to non cooperation and lack of team work in the organisation as a whole.

Ideal attitude at work

In a general sense, the type of ideal situation, condition and attitude that should prevail at the organisation or work place depends on the mentality or consciousness of the working people as given below.

(i)   People should admire that they have got a chance to work for the particular organisation, whereas there are so many people wandering on the roads looking for such an opportunity.

(ii)   The working person should be grateful to his organisation for giving him a position and the required environment. One should feel that he can never pay back for the kind of benefit he has received from the organisation and therefore should render an unconditional service to the organisation.

(iii)   One should not try to injure or cause any difficulty to anyone at the workplace and has to consider colleagues like family members within the organisation.

(iv)   One should feel it as one's responsibility to help the subordinates and peers so that they work to their best for achieving the goals and targets of the organisation.

(v)   As mentioned in the Holy Scriptures, the principle of law of Karma will work and therefore, I should make a perfect balance between what I give to others and what I receive in return from them.

(vi)   Unless I deserve it, nothing can come into my life.

(vii)   Instead of cursing God or your colleagues or to your own self for any of the bad thing happening at your end in the organisation, it is better to think of the basic cause for that undesirable event.

(viii)   As given in the Holy Scriptures, if I discharge my duties properly and correctly without expecting great things in return, all my desires or ambitions will automatically be fulfilled in due course of time.

When we understand and realize the divine support for every aspect of our life, we will be able to observe the harmony and balance between all our thoughts and actions. And importantly, what ever we give or contribute to others will come back to us in manifold ways as being confirmed in the Holy Scriptures.

Integrating spirituality with profession

Adopting the ideal attitude in our profession means taking complete responsibility for everything we render as our occupation. Yoga and meditation will naturally make professionals to have proper spiritual attitude and create the necessary sense of responsibility. This will provide discipline, time consciousness and ability to render hard work and patience within oneself which are lacking now-a-days in highly qualified professionals. The basic purpose of yoga and meditation is to nourish spiritual strength and align mind and senses in the correct direction for performing duties with proper consciousness, dedication and efficiency.

Generally it is observed that when people are inclined towards spirituality, they are more tolerant and at the same time they are peaceful within. These spiritually minded people render more work with high commitment because they are naturally peaceful and happy. When people get affected with negative attitudes, then they render less efficient work to society. Therefore, for having better professional expertise, one should be in constant touch with spirituality and should feel responsible towards their professions.

Steps to make your work as worship

'Work' deals with mundane things like earning money, managing domestic affairs along with satisfying the bodily demands. 'Worship' on the other hand, usually focuses on the divine like offering prayers, meditating and chanting the names of the Lord. Hence, work and worship belong to two distinct domains, one being mundane and other being divine.

On similar grounds, let us analyse the dual dimensions of our human existence which has both material and spiritual parts. As per Holy Scriptures, we are spiritual beings seated as drivers of our vehicle - material body. All living entities including human beings are eternal and beloved children of the Supreme Lord. We must understand that efforts made solely for satisfying the material needs of our body — looking for food, shelter, security along with sense gratification will end up consuming most of our time, whereas not satisfying them will trouble us. But at the same time, only satisfying those will also not bring much fulfilment to our heart and soul.

Being hungry is really a misery, but having food will not always bring joy to our hearts. As we all know, well fed people are not happy always. Food fills our belly but it does not fulfil our heart. Our love hungry hearts can be satisfied only by spiritual love for the Lord. Our human bodies are like vehicles and should be used to elevate our present love for the dead matter to our potential love for the Supreme Lord through the scientific process of devotional service. Therefore, to make work as worship one has to do some spiritual practice everyday. This type of divinely related activity will create a foundation by which we can spiritualize our work for rest of the day. Divinity within us will enable to see all other living beings as fellow family members of God's creation and make our activities as offerings of love to the Lord. Only then will our work become worship and this requires harmonizing our material requirements with spiritual purpose of our lives.

TRUE FRIENDSHIP AND LOVE

This topic on true friendship and love is basically the conversations between Dr. K. Hima Bindu (wife of the author) and friends of her daughter P. Sri Vaishnavi on friendship day at their school. After serving sweet rice as token of love towards the entire class members on this auspicious day, there were discussions with some of the students (who just entered into their teenage). In addition to the points that were discussed the author adds some more additional points based on his views for the benefit of the entire student community.

Three girl students (C1 to C3) along with the daughter (C4) of the couple (Dr. P. Hari Krishna and Dr. Hima Bindu) started their discussions regarding the friendship day.

C1 to C3: Hai aunty, wish you a happy friendship day.

Bindu: Thank you dears. Wish you the same. How do you like the sweet rice.

C1: Yes it is the best of sweet rice I had till now. It is very tasty and so I ask for an extra plate.

C3: Yes aunty, it is very good. Thank you for bringing such a wonderful item for all of us.

C2: Aunty, we four in our class are the best friends.

Bindu: Really. It's good.

C2: Yes aunty, we wish to have our loving friendship always flourishing and we will be good friends for our entire life time.

Bindu: Wonderful. I'm very happy that you all are attending school regularly. Study well. And, it's nice to see you all together as friends. So, today, we'll discuss on friendship and love. OK.

C3: Wow. Sounds great aunty.

Bindu: To make you understand this concept of friendship, I will present my views in the story form to make it interesting.

C1: Stories are my favourite. Thank you.

Bindu: You see, for the humanity, friendship and love are two important necessities in day to day life. Whether a person is a child, young or old aged, these two aspects change his life: by creating either pleasurable and happy or miserable and stressful moments. Some times people get deceived in the name of friendship or love and hence it becomes very important to know about true friendship and love.

Friendship and love should not be a 'one-way traffic', rather it should be a 'two-way traffic' which means that one must be a good friend in order to have good friends and one must love all so that everyone will love him/her in return. To live life fairly, this is a rule that everyone should follow. In other words, if we expect some thing from others, we should be willing to give the same to others. For example, if we expect others to speak only truth to us, we should also speak only truth at all times. Similarly, if one expects good qualities from friends, then one should be ready to practice all those qualities personally. If one can follow this principle, then naturally one can have many wonderful friends and will be loved by all. For understanding these two aspects let us discuss about the true friendship and love in detail.

Who is a friend?

C1: Aunty, I've a question. Who is a friend?

Bindu: Good, I was just coming to it. A friend is someone whose company others can enjoy. And very importantly a friend not only enjoys your good times, but also supports you when you are in trouble or in difficult situations. In the present day society, we find that when a person is going through a good period in his/her life, everyone flocks around him/her. But we cannot say all of them are good friends. The best example we can have for this situation is the condition of a wealthy person. For a wealthy person, many people will try to be around, who may not be true well-wishers or friends. In the true sense, those who stay by us in bad times also are true friends; as the famous proverb goes...

C4: "A friend in need is a friend indeed."

Bindu: Very good, that's right.

Important qualities of good friendship

C3: I would like to know about the important qualities of good friendship

Bindu: There are three very important qualities, which we have to cultivate to make good friendship.

1. Loyalty: Loyalty in friendship means maintaining one's dignity in the relationship without intending to back stab. Loyalty towards our friend is necessary when others attack our friend in any situation. We should not take back when our friend is in need of us. In other words, friendship cannot be turned on and off as if it were a radio set or an electrical switch, depending on the circumstances and needs.
2. Sincerity: For long lasting friendship, sincerity is very important. People in general trust those who are honest about their ideas and feelings. The lack of sincerity in one's actions will result in destroying the confidence and damages the friendship.
3. Trust worthiness: Trust worthiness in friendship means keeping one's own words or promises. One should know how to keep important and personal things secret. In case the friend comes to know that the confidential issues are distorted, then one's reputation as a trustable person is lost.

One should choose own friends carefully so that he will be in a good company of friendship. In general, we feel like doing whatever our friends do. One may be balanced, well-behaved, confident and honest, but if he/she gets into a bad company of people, he is bound to get affected and develop bad habits. Many times, this is one of the main reasons why children from good families develop bad habits and indulge in improper ways of living. If we recall a popular saying that 'You can tell about a man from the type of friends or company of people he has', which indicates that one's behaviour will be decided by the type of friends he/she cultivates. Also we know that 'Birds of same feather flock together', which means that in general people with similar kind of behaviour will stay together.

Generally, one can be more relaxed with a good friend than with people one does not know well. But in life, it is not correct to take a person for granted. In the society, no body wants his/her feelings to be hurt. One should be sensitive, thoughtful and considerate towards his friends to have good relationships. Every human being has some or the other faults; needless to say no one is perfect in behaviour, including yourself and your friend. Hence one should be liberal in overlooking some of the faults in friends.

Real Friend

C2: Aunty, you said you'll tell stories. Can you tell a story about a real friend?

Bindu: You've reminded me about it, smart girl. A real friend is one who comes to you with love and cheer when all others have left you behind alone. Such a friend is discovered not by your search for the right person to become a friend but by your sincere endeavour to become the right person to deserve a friend. Naturally, a question arises in one's mind – who is our nearest friend? Not surely a neighbour or bench mate at school, or our family members, but He is God. God is seated as super soul in the heart of every living being. God reveals in the Holy Scriptures that it is He, Himself who is the actual well-wisher and benefactor of every living being, including animals, plants, humans etc. In Sanskrit, *Mitra* is a special friend and *bandhu* is an official friend, but *suhrt* is a heart to heart friend. *Suhrt* is such a wonderful friend that even if you harm your friend he cannot think/do harm for you.

For example, a child may demand a food item surrounded by flies in an unhygienic condition, but his/her parents would deny providing that type of food. The child may cry or may punch on his parents' faces; the parents will surely tolerate the punch of child with a smile. Later they take the child to a nice place or inside their own house to provide wonderful food items which are prepared nicely in a hygienic condition. Similarly, even if we don't bother about the Lord, He is always taking care of all our needs like a father/mother. He is seated in the heart of every living being as *paramatma* or supersoul.

It's observed that people are ready to do good to you as long as you don't cause any trouble to them; but the Supreme Lord and His representatives have one nature in common – they always do 'good' to all living entities. We learn from the Bible that when Jesus was crucified on the cross, he prayed to God saying "O Lord! Do not punish them, for they know not what they do."

From this example we understand that the Lord and His representatives like Jesus, Prophet Mohammed and some others are the true friends of the society. To understand the Lord's mercy better, let's take one example from the Srimad Bhagavatam. As she wanted, I'll tell you the story of true eternal friendship between the Supreme Lord Sri Krishna and Sudama.

Example of True Friendship

Thousands of years ago, the society was guided by an intelligent class of men called Brahmanas. They helped others in their search for truth and devoted every word, thought, and deed to the service of Lord.

Sudama was a kind and gentle Brahmin who used to perform his priestly duties in a regulated manner. He used to read from scriptures, chanted sacred mantras and taught everyone in his small village how to lead a holy life. Sudama was wise and self-controlled and saw all living creatures as equal. However, in his middle age became very poor. The only clothes he and his good wife along with children owned were old and worn, and because their food was meagre, they looked thin and weak. Even though, Sudama was not interested in material pleasures or wealth, he always remained peaceful and happy despite his poverty. But, his wife was worried about his health. One day, she told her beloved husband, "I am very concerned about your and our children's well-being. Please go to your friend Krishna, who is now the King of Dwaraka. As children you both have studied together in the same school. Surely He knows how dear you are to Him and how much you are determined to instruct others about spiritual life. If you ask, He will not hesitate to help you obtain the bare necessities in life."

But Sudama was not at all anxious to ask Krishna about any personal favours. He thought in a different way "If I go to Dwaraka, I shall see my dear friend again which will be wonderful." So he agreed to his wife's plan and asked her to prepare a small gift for his friend Krishna. As they were very poor she could not find any gift other than four palms full of chipped rice from their neighbours and tied it in a small cloth. It was humble and that was all that they had. Sudama took that gift and left for the royal city of Dwaraka.

During the journey, walking, Sudama recollected his childhood adventures with Krishna, when they stayed in the Gurukula of Sandipani Muni. One day, Krishna and Sudama went to the forest to collect firewood for their guru, and by chance they lost their way. At that time there was a huge storm along with thunders and harsh winds. Acting like an ordinary child, Krishna spent the entire night with his friend in the forest itself taking shelter under a big tree.

The next morning, Sandipani Muni along with his other students who came to the forest in search of Krishna and Sudama, located them under the tree. The Muni said, "My dear students, you have suffered so much trouble just for me. This is the proof of how serious you are to serve your master." He blessed them saying, "May all your desires be fulfilled and may you always remember the teachings of the scriptures. Thus you will be happy both in this life and in the next."

Remembering these types of events, Sudama marvelled at Krishna's humility and wondered, "Although Krishna is the source of all knowledge, yet He accepted a spiritual master and went to the school just to set an example for children everywhere."

After arriving at Dwaraka, Sudama walked through the big gates and beautiful gardens in the palace of Krishna which were protected by guards everywhere. He also walked though the arches of regal palaces and then came to the most splendid palace of all. Inside, Lord Krishna was spending time with His beautiful queen, Rukmini. As soon as Sudama arrived, Krishna came running to embrace him with great affection. Krishna invited Sudama to sit on His own bed and brought him fruits and drinks. He washed Sudama's feet and sprinkled the water on His own head as a sign of great respect towards his friend. Then He applied Sandalwood paste on Sudama's body to cool him after the journey.

Meanwhile, Queen Rukmini fanned Sudama with a yak-tail fan. After offering royal welcome and after Sudama had honoured food and drinks, Krishna said, "My dear friend, it is a great fortune that you have come here." The Brahmana, being very poor, was not dressed nicely; his clothing was torn and dirty, and his body was also very lean and thin. Because of his weak body, his bones were distinctly visible. While the goddess of fortune, Laxmi Devi, in the form of Rukmini, personally fanned him, the other women in the palace were astonished to see the manner in which Krishna received the poor Brahmana.

They were surprised to see that the Brahmana seated on the bedstead of Lord Krishna and even more surprised to see the Lord embraced him exactly the same way as He would embrace His elder brother, Lord Balaram.

Such a fashion of embrace was done by Lord Krishna only with Rukmini and Balarama, and no one else.

Krishna was glad to see Sudama after so many years, and together they chatted about many things. Krishna said to his friend, "It is rare to find a good friend like you, so detached from the material world.

Smiling, He asked Sudama, "Do you have a present for me?"

Sudama hesitated to answer Krishna.

Then Krishna says, "My dear friend, I certainly do not need anything, but a gift of love from My good friend, even a small gift, brings Me great pleasure".

Sensing that Sudama was embarrassed to give Him that small bundle of chipped rice, Krishna snatched the bag containing chipped rice and said, "Wow? It is delicious chipped rice! Such a gift will not only satisfy me, but also the whole universe!"

Lord Krishna, who is accustomed to receiving millions of tasty offerings every day in temples around the world, ate one morsel of chipped rice and felt completely satisfied.

Krishna invited Sudama to spend the night at His palace. The next morning, after paying his respects to Lord Krishna, Sudama left Dwaraka.

"How fortunate I am", he thought, "Lord Krishna embraces the goddess of fortune, yet He also embraced a poor Brahmin like me. He made me sit on His own bed, fed me, and massaged my legs. He considered me to be like His own brother. And Queen Rukmini was fanning me! What more, He was so kind that He did not flatter me with riches. He knows I would become puffed up by wealth and soon forget Him."

Thinking so, he reached home. But he was surprised by seeing the condition of his house. He found that this was not the same home he had left from. Everything looked changed. In place of his cottage stood palaces made of marble, precious stones and gems. There were beautiful parks and lakes filled with lotus flowers. He thought "May be this is the wrong house." At that moment he saw his wife, dressed like the goddess of fortune herself. As she saw him, tears of joy dropped down her eyes; together, they entered their palace. Sudama gazed at the columns which were embellished with jewels, gems, golden thrones along with emerald carvings. He was surprised, but realized that these were gifts from his dear friend, Krishna. He said to himself, "Krishna took one morsel of broken rice and in exchange has given me all this. Let me not become proud, since I am not the real owner of this wealth. It belongs to Him, the supreme person, who has created it. It shall be used for His service and all that I truly desire for myself is His friendship."

Even after being given so much wealth, Sudama remained humble, a friend to everyone and forever devoted to the Supreme Lord, Krishna. Thus Sudama, the wise Brahmin, saw the entire creation as the property of the Supreme Lord and was thus a truly wealthy man.

Could you understand this story. Can anyone say the essence of this story.

C4: Lord is our best friend

Bindu: Yes, Correct. If you consider the Supreme Personality of Godhead Sri Krishna as your best and intimate friend, then the Lord will surely reciprocate in a way more than we can not even imagine or expect.

C2: Thank you aunty; that was a very interesting story. So, how do we maintain friends as good as Krishna and Sudama were, to each other?

Bindu: I'm glad you liked the story. Now, let us discuss the important points to maintain the true friendship with others.

1. True friendship is very important in everyone's life. The whole world is heading fast in a false direction. People think "If you do this for me, I will do this for you" or "As long as I have something to get from you, you are my good friend, once my work or business is over, I have nothing to give and take with you." But, to experience true friendship there should be a strong bond of love and trust between friends.

2. We can develop love among our friends by giving gifts, accepting gifts, by revealing our mind in confidence, by hearing in confidence from them, by accepting food and by offering food at home.

3. In one's life, one should at least have few friends with whom he/she can share their joys and sorrows, which cannot be shared with everyone alike.

4. We should also have intimate friends who will not fear to boldly correct our mistakes. And similarly we should have such friends who can joke with us and make our heart feel light whenever we are not in a good mood. Similarly, we can share our problems and weaknesses with good friends who can help us directly or indirectly.

What is Love?

C3: We hope we get to experience such good friendship with each other. You also said you would talk about love. What exactly is it aunty?

Bindu: Today, love is one of the most popular and most frequently used terms especially by teenagers like you but the least understood too. Because, love is equated with sensual enjoyment and mostly related to the beauty aspect; sadly, such a superficial titillation doesn't offer the required satisfaction for the heart. Although people have recognized the hunger of the belly for nutritious food, they have not recognized the hunger of the heart for true love.

Today, the universal attractive principle in this entire world is beauty, and only beauty. Most often, people are instantly attracted to anything and everything that is beautiful. But, as per the Holy Scriptures, all the beauty in this world is not true; in other words it means that it will be painfully fleeting, for some months or years only. Beauty has no truth in it, in the sense that while at one moment a certain thing appears beautiful, few moments later the same beauty in the same item may vanish. Therefore, one may doubt whether there is compatibility between truth and beauty. There is a saying that truth is not always beautiful; rather it is often unpleasant and discouraging.

According to Scriptures, truth is absolute and always beautiful. This truth is so beautiful that it attracts everyone: eminent personalities, sages, saints etc... Dedicated devotees of the Lord have left everything for the sake of this absolute truth. We can take the example of the father of our nation, Mahatma Gandhi in this regard, who dedicated his life to experiment with truth. It is said that the absolute truth is not only all-beautiful, but also all-powerful, all-resourceful, all-famous, all-renounced and all-knowledgeable.

Hari Krishna Padavala

True Love Means To Give

C1: Mahatma Gandhi symbolizes sacrifice. He sacrificed his life for his countrymen, to achieve independence for the country from British rule. So, does true love mean sacrifice?

Bindu: You see, since time immemorial, the essential need for every living being is to seek pleasure. As we can observe from nature, different types of living entities set varying standards for pleasure and will work in different ways to achieve them. For example, an ant will derive pleasure in getting a grain of sugar and will work so hard to get the same even by risking its life. Among humans, some people derive pleasure by inflicting pain and harming others while some others derive from being famous and being adored and worshipped. Many derive great pleasure in acquiring wealth, property and the power that comes along with these. On the other hand, in nature we also find a mother deriving pleasure in giving satisfaction to her child, while a father seeks pleasure in seeing the family prospering nicely.

In this way, everyone seeks pleasure and the most fundamental form is the pleasure of love, without which no living entity can sustain life. For example, if you were the proprietor of the entire universe but the only person on the same universe, certainly you will be the unhappy person. In other words, one can not feel real satisfaction or happiness in the heart without people to love and at the same time without being loved. Today, the real problem troubling people is the poverty of the heart and the only way to quench that hunger is to love.

The only thing that touches the heart of any living being is love and really speaking to love means to give. For understanding this principle let us take an example of real pleasure of a mother. As such the child gives nothing to the mother, but the mother is found to get more satisfaction in that child than practically anything else and all that she does is giving her love, sacrificing. When we have a little baby in the house, some times there is practically no peace in the house. The baby may be crying all night, attending to natural calls, indiscriminately, wherever it goes. Although the baby creates so much inconvenience, the mother runs here and there, taking good care of the child. Hence we understand that here love is higher than peace and it is not to take, but to give. The more you give and the more genuine your giving is, the more people naturally reciprocate, thus bringing satisfaction to the heart.

Smiling Faces but Crying Empty Hearts

C2: Yes Aunty, my mother loves me and I love her more than that. Another short story, please.

Bindu: The mother-child relationship is based on unconditional love, yes. Being a doctor I will try to explain this point in medical terms.

A patient, suffering from severe pain in his body, consulted a doctor. The latter prescribed an expensive antibiotic and a cheap pain killer. The patient accidentally discovered that taking the pain killer is enough to keep the pain away; he felt happy and thought he need not spend more money on the treatment. Sadly here the patient is not aware of what would happen to the pain once he stops taking pain killers. They just create an illusion in the mind: of reduction in pain externally. But, internally, the disease worsens in the body and naturally will become aggravated to such a level that the pain killer would no longer work. By that time, the situation may get worst that even the antibiotic would not be able to cure the disease.

In the present day situation, our heart is really seeking love and the happiness that it gives. Naturally loving relationships provide meaning and joy to life. Sometimes such relationships make our life worth living for amidst the hardships we face day in and day out. Sometimes, the intimate relationships, which have the potential of bringing the highest happiness, may turn to be sources of our anxiety and agony. Being an extremely intense emotion, love builds for the object of love such a high tower of expectation, hope and dreams that is practically impossible for any human being to ascend and stay at that tower.

Many times, it is seen that if some how a satisfying loving relationship gets developed between two people, it may get severed in some time. The intensity of agony in the pain that ensues is directly proportional to the strength of the relationship. Some people, at the risk of facing such hardships, keep themselves away from such loving relationships. But when a person does not have loving relationships at all, then his/her heart will profoundly get empty and makes life seem dry, bereft of the purpose and boring. Many people are seen living with this type of heart disease, their hearts longing for loving relationships with the desire for happiness from them.

Although the advancement in science and technology could increase physical comforts and luxuries by creating many electronic gadgets, it cannot fill the empty hearts of people. The mechanical life style reduces the strength of relationships and takes a toll on our behaviour as well. To modern man, the term 'love' is bandied word especially in the media, but what is portrayed as love is sadly not true love but lust.

Love and Lust: What Is The Difference

C4: Mama, I am getting confused here. Can you please explain the differences between love and lust?

Bindu: Yes dear. The tragedy of the modern society is that it also gets confused just like you and is unable to understand the difference between love and lust. Many times, in the name of love, people are carried away with the dangerous 'lust'. Now let us discuss the difference between them. Actually, they are totally different from each other, say like opposite poles, but is seldom understood by many people. A lusty person sees the other one as an object for one's own enjoyment in terms of sex, whereas a person who loves the other wants to serve and to please. In the present day advanced way of life style with rampant obscenity in movies and pornography, people are more inclined to get bodily satisfaction in terms of sex. A Holy Scripture compares love with the precious gold where as lust is like copper. If copper is gold-coated, an unintelligent and uninformed person mistakes the same to be gold.

Lust originates from the fundamental ignorance of our own identity. When we mistake ourselves to be the outwardly seen physical body, whether it is in a male or female form, we naturally come under the influence of lusty pleasure. Lust leads to hunger for matter within one, and this precisely is what people struggle intensely to fulfil; by exploiting another person's body for this lusty pleasure. In material world, men treat women like sex machine whereas women treat men like ATM machine. We see and hear incidents wherein a boy claims to love a girl, but if she rejects his proposal, he takes revenge on the same girl by throwing acid on her face or by stabbing her leading to her death. Similarly, a girl claims to love a boy, but if she finds a richer person who can give her more comforts and facilities, she leaves her so-called 'heartthrob'. When relationships are based on this lust, as is happening in the so-called 'love marriages', they lead to frustration and end in divorces. By such examples, we may doubt why 'love', which appears to be a wonderful romance before marriage, results in violence after marriage. Is this the love which the people dream for? Certainly not, it is just lust in the name of love.

Now-a-days colleges and universities, especially in the western countries, are offering courses on sex, where in they educate people on how to improve sexual potency. As such no living entity needs any education to have sex; it's one that naturally arises on attainment of a certain age (puberty) just like all of you. In the previous ages, through Vedic education, apart from teaching students commercial, technical and physical skills, gurus / teachers used to focus on imparting knowledge about the philosophical understanding of one's spiritual identity so that they would not be victimised by the passions of sex. Basically, sex is a bodily drive, which occurs to a person after a particular age (as mentioned earlier as puberty) to facilitate procreation. Vedic education, far more sophisticated than modern education, recognized that the consciousness of the man and the woman at the time of union is very important to determine the nature of the soul to enter the mother's womb.

In olden days, cognisant of this rich fundamental knowledge, a newly married couple would enter into sexual intercourse not just for sexual enjoyment but to offer great services to the family in particular and the society at large, by giving birth to a good soul. The prospective parents were educated on the great responsibility associated with the upbringing of a child in this world, who would eventually become an exemplary, principled and selfless citizen in the society. Thus in Vedic times, sex was not meant for recreation but for procreation. In the modern times, people are scientifically suppressing procreation in terms of contraception and abortion, so as to yield for more recreation. The famous Beatle, John Lenon was once quoted as saying, "most people take their seed in their mother's womb on Saturday nights over a bottle of wine."

The sanctified marriage ceremony is meant for gratification of one's bodily sexual drive in a regulated and religious way to seek a sanctified procreation. This type of consciousness of both the husband and the wife help them to realize the futility of bodily enjoyment and help each other to advance together on the journey back to God. As stated by one of the great personality, "marriage is meant to regulate the human mind so that it becomes peaceful for spiritual advancement." Therefore, the purpose of marriage is not only to facilitate bodily sense gratification but for spiritual purification as well.

Message of Love

C3: That was so detailed. What do the scriptures talk about true love?

Bindu: Many eminent people and scholars like Mahatma Gandhi, Albert Einstein, Ralph Waldo Emerson and Henry David Thoreau have praised and followed the Scriptures. The hidden message of true love towards God, which is the conclusion of the Scriptures, is the most essential healing technique required for the present misdirected love-starved society. In this great scripture, the message of love is mentioned as: 'We (all living entities) are spirit souls, entitled to rejoice the eternal love with the supremely lovable and loving God. In contrast, when our loving nature is contaminated with selfishness, we start loving things around us more than the people around us and even God. This misdirected love towards useless material things makes us to identify with the temporary bodily coverings and impels us to exploit others for our own sense enjoyment'.

A doctor who is well wishing friend of his patients is at times forced to perform a surgery on them though he doesn't want to cause pain to the patient. The idea is to save the patient and not punish him. Similarly, Lord Krishna instructed Arjuna to surgically heal Duryodhana's selfishness mentality on the battlefield of Kurukshetra.

Each one of us has the mentalities of both Arjuna and Duryodhana in our hearts. And the scriptures like Bhagavad-Gita teaches us to become spiritual warriors to conquer the selfish lower self with the selfless attitude of higher self. Just like how this message of the Bhagavad-Gita empowered Arjuna, it can empower us too, for seek love in our hearts, to family members; to the society we live in and to the world at large.

In the conclusion of this scripture, Lord Krishna expresses his love for Arjuna by saying "Because you are My dear friend, I am speaking to you My supreme instruction which is the most confidential knowledge in the entire creation – Always think of Me, become My devotee, worship Me and offer your homage unto Me and by doing so you will surely come to Me without fail. I promise you about this important aspect because you are My very dear friend."

Further, Krishna instructs Arjuna to "Abandon all varieties of religion and just surrender unto Me. I shall deliver you from all sinful reactions, do not fear about this." Through the Bhagavad Gita, Lord Krishna advocates the non-sectarian belief in terms of universal spiritual love. He is not only teaching this aspect of love, but is also demonstrating the same by happily accepting to take a menial role of charioteer or driver of Arjuna on the battle field.

As George Harrison, the main member of the Beatles group in UK expressed, "God is who loves those who love Him."

When we choose the path of love as revealed in this Holy Scripture, He in turn reciprocates by illuminating our heart with divine wisdom and spiritual love. Thus, the Bhagavad-Gita is essentially a revelation of divinity's love for entire humanity as well as a love call for humanity's reciprocal love for the divinity.

Let all of us, including you, your friends, your family members, neighbours and tomorrow your children, tread this path of love and simultaneously let us love all living beings in the entire creation and then be loved by all.

C1: Thank you aunty for coming here and talking to us.

C3: Yes aunty, we really learnt a lot from you.

C2: We sincerely promise that we will practise in life all that we have learnt from you today.

C4: Bye mama. I am so happy that you are my sweet mother.

Bindu: I feel happy to have talked with you all for so long my friends. All the best. May God bless you all with true friendship among all of you.

DEALING WITH HABITS

Mr. M.V. Srikanth, an alumni of National Institute of Technology, Warangal presently working as Manager in a leading oil company in Hyderabad, visits his institute by accompanying his daughter who wish to participate in Technozion program conducted at the institute every year. Technozion is a technical fest aiming at providing a platform for all the professional students from different colleges like IIT's, NIT's along with other universities in the entire country to participate and share their technical capabilities. Approximately more than 4,500 students from different colleges of the country will participate in the programs during this event.

While looking at the young students in action, he is intrigued by their behaviour and found certain things missing in them. This leads him to contemplate on 'habits' and how they shape an individual, cutting across age groups, social strata, race and cultures. Thus follows an interesting conversation as he chances upon his friend Dr. P. Hari Krishna, faculty member of the institute.

Srikanth: Hai Hari, how are you man? How is your life interms of family and profession?

Hari: Thank you Srikanth. I am fine, doing well in life. It's nice that I could meet you after a long time after our college studies. I welcome you back to our institution.

Srikanth: I'm overwhelmed by looking at these students in their technical skills. It's a wonderful feeling and I deeply appreciate this initiative by our college in terms of opting for this type of technical fest which will surely help these young professionals to present the principles what they are studying to practical applications.

Hari: I appreciate your observation. Actually, we are thankful to parents like you who bring or send their children here and provide us with an opportunity to conduct such a magnificient event for the benefit of the entire society.

Srikanth: Looking at these students together takes me to our own student days in this campus. These events really make the present day professional students to learn and coordinate among themselves in terms of team work in learning, understanding and applying their technical knowledge to the benefit of the society and nation.

Hari: Yes, I truly agree with you.

Habits

Srikanth: That drives me to ask you; in today's society, it is well known that habits of a person will lead one's life in two directions – either peaceful and happy or miserable and unhappy. While I agree this topic is essential for the entire humanity, it is important for the young generation in particular, as they are the most effected. We find youth during their college days in addition to acquiring their professional knowledge are indulging in unhealthy activities like smoking cigarettes, consuming alcohol, taking to drugs and pandering to other types of illicit activities, not just because they want to do it, but because they want to appear cool and be accepted by the people around them to be heroic. Can you throw some light on it by saying about habits?

Hari: Sure. Habit is defined as something that you do repeatedly or regularly. The Oxford dictionary defines habit as the activity which has got settled in our mind or has a regular tendency to be repeated; the one activity that is practiced for some time and becomes hard to give-up; it is also considered as the mental constitution or attitude of the person.

In this entire creation, every one of us has the wonderful gift called as 'free will' provided by the Supreme Lord and we have to choose between good and bad at every moment in life. Let's take the example of Mr. Edward; although the King of England, he had the habit of stealing small things from different people. Of course, he did such type of activity because of a psychological disease he suffered from, called 'Cliptomenia'. He got addicted to such a bad habit because of his inability to control himself and thus felt really embarrassed.

Simple, Serious and Grave bad habits

Let us take a look into some of the simple and serious bad habits.

Simple bad habits: The activities like biting nails, laughing at inappropriate times, eating and sleeping too much, gossiping about unnecessary things and useless people, postponing things due to laziness, poking into others' affairs frequently, passing rumours about others, addiction to coffee or tea etc.

Serious bad habits: As you rightly mentioned earlier, addiction to smoking, drinking alcohol, drugs, indulging in gambling activities etc.

Grave bad habits: Making illicit connections with many women; stealing and robbery, forgery, murder, terrorism etc.

How are Habits Addictive?

Srikanth: I like this categorisation that you have done. But what intrigues me is how they become so addictive that we feel compelled to keep doing them time and again.

Hari: Let us analyse the example of smoking of cigarettes by any person out of his own free will. In the early days, it tastes horrible to smoke a cigarette, but when he keeps doing it until he becomes habituated to surrendering to that experience, in due course of time, he becomes addicted to it and it thus becomes as a habit. By this type of addiction, he is being forced to think in the initial days that "I have to do it and after some period I have to do it anyway"; later he will surely think that

"I must do it"; further he will reach a stage when he feels that "I cannot live without it". Similar is the case with other addictions like alcoholism and drug addiction.

In this regard, if we look at the word of "HABIT" —

When we remove 'H' what remains is 'A BIT',
and when we remove 'H' and 'A', what remains is 'BIT'
and when we remove 'H', 'A' and 'B', still what remains is 'IT'.

Similarly, the habits have a nature to make us get addicted to them and will not leave us easily for a long period of time. Hence, we have to understand certain important facts about habits, which I shall now share.

(i) Old habits die hard. Habits are first cobwebs, and then will become cables.
(ii) Habits are like soft cosy beds – easy to get in, difficult to get out.
(iii) Cultivating a habit is like ploughing a field.
(iv) Habits start by being too weak to be 'felt', and end up becoming too strong to be 'left'.
(v) Before you realize that you have to get the habit, the habits have got you.

What are the causes of addicting to Bad habits?

Srikanth: That was really well put. This is something we do in the Corporate as well. Breaking a problem into smaller elements and structuring them well. Coming back, what really causes addiction to bad habits?

Hari: In nature, living beings get lured by one or the other way. For example, a fish may be lured by the worm on the hook of the fisherman; similarly a mouse is lured by the cheese in the mouse-trap. These two examples show how living beings get trapped into dangerous situations and even invite death because of their struggle for existence and the desire for sustenance. If we go deeper, both the fish and mouse have excuses like

(i)   They were initially not aware of the fact that they were going to get trapped once they bite either the worm or cheese and

(ii)   They were in want of food for their sustenance.

But in the case of human beings, although people are aware of the consequences, he/she gets trapped into many dangerous situations like getting addicted to smoking, alcohol, drugs, stealing, forgery, illicit relationships etc. and therefore invite unhealthy conditions and invite death in their lives.

Let's analyse the statistics and facts about smoking tobacco as furnished by World Health Organization.

(i)   Tobacco kills around 10,000 people worldwide every day.

(ii)   It is predicted that by the year 2020, the tobacco use will cause about 12% of all the deaths globally. This number of deaths is more than the combined deaths due to HIV, Tuberculosis, accidents, suicides, maternal mortality etc.

(iii)   It is found that half of the people, who start smoking during the young age will die in the middle age only, losing around 22 years of normal life of expectancy.

(iv)   It is a hard fact that an average cigarette contains about 400 poisonous substances and more than 40 cancer causing chemicals.

(v)   The statistics say that about one third of the entire global population who are aged around 15 years and above is smoking cigarettes regularly.

Similarly, the other major factor that disturbs the young generation is attraction to sex. One of the students asked the great scholar Pythogoras, "When should one have sex in the life?" The great man replied, "Whenever you wish to be weaker than yourself, you may have it" This quite clearly indicates the disadvantage of indulging in sex unnecessarily. In their teens, both boys and girls are greatly forced to this great attraction and are involved in this natural act before they even finish their education.

The research by Dr. R.W. Bernard as published in his article on "Science Discovers the Physiological Value of Continence" concludes in terms of power of semen of human beings that 'an ounce of semen is considered to be equivalent to about 60 ounces of blood', Therefore, wastage of semen from one's body will generally be accompanied by the loss of precious proteins and minerals and further it will reduce the vitality and immunity of human beings. In this regard, the French philosopher Auguste Comte mentions that 'to control the sexual urge for the humans in an efficient manner has always been found to be the highest test of wisdom.' Even from an intellectual point, great scholars like Aristotle, Beethoven, Leonardo da Vinci, Pythagoras and Sir Isaac Newton have taken up celibacy to convert their sexual energy into intellectual insights.

From a spiritual perspective, as mentioned in scriptures, we are transmigrating through many species, as the spirit souls taking different shapes and have had the experience of this great alluring act of indulging in sex for momentary happiness for the past many life times. When we are in this great and special human form, we have the wonderful opportunity to seek the spiritual aspect of life and thus attaining eternal happiness – a great privilege that no other form of species is being offered. Let's try to analyse and understand how this natural act of having sex is becoming a big hurdle or problem in the present day human society.

What's bad is many young and intelligent students invest their most valuable time during their college days to learn and experience this luring aspect of having sex either with opposite gender; now-a-days sometimes even with the same gender. Even students belong to premier institutes like the IITs and the NITs are found misusing the internet facility, provided for the sake of doing academic research, to download the pictures and videos of pornography. Surprisingly some of the institutes or universities in the western countries impart sex education in their course curriculum in the name of educating the younger generation. In reality there is absolutely no necessity for any education to learn about sex. In nature, all the animals, birds and aquatics are indulging in this natural phenomenon without studying any theory or practice.

In a similar vein, we have seen such self-destructive behavioural aspects in alcoholism and other bad habits. And surprisingly, even the so called normal people are victimized by some or other forms of self-destructive behavioural patterns like unwarranted expression of anger that may lead to disastrous situations or incidents.

Hence, a question will arise in our minds about how an intelligent man can take such a self-destructive course in life. Most of the times, people very well know that they are treading the danger zone when they first indulge; besides, they also find the statutory warning imposed by the Government printed on cigarette packets: Cigarette smoking is injurious to health. However, due to the influence of friends and media propaganda, they want to experiment. Generally, the instant pleasure impression gets embedded in the minds of people and whenever they find a situation calling for some immediate pleasure to counteract another situation, they recall this smoking pleasure and resort to it; the process continues without intervention by their own intelligence and with time, becomes unmitigated. Therefore, this smoking habit becomes an irresistible demand for the mind and further turns out to be a compulsive need; in other words, an addiction.

How some habits are bad though they feel good?

Srikanth: I find one particular aspect of your talk interesting. That is, how some habits, although bad, makes us feel good about them.

Hari: A very deep question, indeed. One has to understand that some habits are really bad, although they may provide momentary pleasure. But these types of bad habits will surely affect our destiny in due course of time. In this regard, there is a saying that

> Sow a thought – Reap an action
> Sow an action – Reap a habit
> Sow a habit – Reap a character
> Sow a character – Reap a destiny.

It's a fact that out of the three main requirements for humans — character, health and wealth — the most important is 'character' which will naturally provide the required health and also provide the necessary wealth. But today's society is heading very fast in the direction of acquiring more wealth thereby losing their health and also not recognising the importance of exhibiting proper character.

Let us make an attempt to understand the consequences of indulging in some bad habits; say for example, intoxication. Intoxication through different forms like alcohol, drugs etc. is found to result in lowering the levels of intelligence. It takes one through an upward kick or pleasure and then takes us towards downward depression. This momentary kick makes the person to get addicted to that intoxication and in due course of time eventually robs him off good health and finally leads to death. It maddens one's mind and increases slavery tendency to the senses which may lead to dangerous consequences. Therefore, this feeling of getting a momentary pleasure by taking to intoxicants will result in addiction to these habits and makes the person behave in an inhuman way. Similar is the case with other things like gambling, meat eating, illicit sex etc.

What impels one to go on with a bad habit?

It is a fact that the sub-conscious mind of a human being is like a BOOK. By changing the SCRIPTS written in the BOOK of our sub-conscious mind, we can change our conditioning and habits. Therefore, one who has interest in changing himself with regard to bad habits should try to change the SCRIPTS in his sub-conscious mind i.e. BOOK. Now, let us try to understand the means to achieve such a change in the SCRIPTS in the BOOK.

(i)   The kind of BOOKS we read matter; for example if we read pornography related books, our mind will get driven towards sexual thoughts, whereas if we read the books on morals, value adding spiritual books like the Ramayana, the Bhagavad-Gita, the Bible, the Quran etc. then our mind will try to acquire more knowledge to control the mind against such tendencies for sense gratification.

(ii)   The kind of MOVIES / VIDEOS we see, either sex related films or value adding movies will have everlasting impressions in the mind.

(iii)   The kind of MUSIC we listen, either biological-rhythm disturbing music like rock or soothing classical music.

(iv)   The kind of FRIENDS we keep; either the ones who drag us into the zone of bad habits or those who elevate our consciousness.

However our consciousness is what our way of thinking is; we should understand that it is not our constitutional position; it is our acquired nature, based on living conditions and the people whom we are associated with. It is nature of the characteristics that we have created ourselves according to what and whom we choose to associate with in our lives – either in this life or from our previous lives.

When we associate with people who are positive and when we choose to engage in a positive perspective with positive activities, then we recondition ourselves in that positive way. This is the special virtue of human life – that we always have the freedom of choice. You may not be able to control the environment but you have full control of how you are going to react to the environment. For example, if you wish to travel on a boat, you may not have control over which way the wind blows, but you do have control over the sails of your boat and how you are going to respond. So you have a choice to choose. Similarly, when unpleasant and unfair things come upon us, we can either choose to complain the same to others or we can learn a lesson from that incident.

How to have the right perception?

Srikanth: This is a subject matter widely discussed in the corporate as well – how to deal with a slow economy, dip in production and quarterly profits, strikes in factories, external factors affecting the industry and problems are aplenty in the world. While I've been part of a lot of such seminars, I would like to hear from you on how to have the right perception of things.

Hari: Human intelligence needs to be properly utilized to see the positive side of any situation. You may be aware that the Bible says "Knock and the door will open for you." Every situation in life is an opportunity and most people complain about the noise when ever the opportunity knocks the door. Hence in every situation, people should be able to see the positive possibilities that come upon us in our daily life.

For example, one person may say "Look at this rosebush, it is full of thorns." He keeps grumbling about the thorns on the rose bush. Another person rejoices, "Look at this thorn bush; it has a rose in it." While both of them saw the same thing, they see it differently. It is like you have rose-coloured glasses, everything will look rose coloured only. If you have yellow-coloured glasses, everything will look yellow. Whereas if you have clear glasses, you see everything as it is. So according to our state of consciousness, we develop certain types of attitudes; we perceive reality according to our acquired attitudes. What type of attitude we choose to adopt in a situation is what will determine our consciousness and our perception of the world we live in.

Therefore, it is a general finding that what ever goes into our system must emit the same thing in due course of time, which is called as GIGO principle. If we consider two examples of

a) The condition of any vehicle depends on how the driver handles it.
b) The beauty of any garden depends on the care and attention of the gardener who handles it.

Similarly, it depends on us (the soul), how dirty or pure our mind is going to be because we are the ones who take in inputs from books, movies, music, friends etc. If we choose to give good input, we will also be able to give good output.

- Garbage IN – Garbage OUT
- Positivity IN – Positivity OUT
- Negativity IN – Negativity OUT
- Good IN – Good OUT

How to say 'NO' to Bad Habits?

Srikanth: Certainly a detailed explanation it was. But, what I would like to know more on is how one says a strong 'NO' to Bad Habits.

Hari: Of course, if people were better educated about the dangers involved in getting addicted to these habits, would it deter them from addictive indulgences? This may happen some times, but not for everyone every time. Some times it may have opposite effect also. For example, the Government has made it mandatory to display the statutory warning on cigarettes: 'Cigarette smoking is injurious to health' on every cigarette pack but the sales of cigarettes are only increasing. Thus, sometimes the warnings tend to evoke a daredevil spirit in people to experience the same restricted act.

In practice, the two SS formula may work nicely to avoid getting indulged in bad habits.

(1) Starve the Bad Habits – If you abstain from the alluring objects and bad company, then naturally there is starving for such habits and with time they die down.

(2) Supplement the Good Habits – If one can stay with people of good character, good objects and good environment, then one can seek introspection into what he is doing and thus develop self-correction for any mistakes or errors.

The Power of Good Habits

Srikanth: (Smiles) I reserve this SS formula for my next presentation when such a topic arises. (Looking at the watch) I think I took too much of your time. But, just before I leave, I would like to dwell on the positive side. I would like to hear from you on the power of good habits.

Hari: The intelligence aspect in humans is powerful in controlling oneself from getting addicted to bad things. And basically the intelligence of humans has two functions:

1. **Discrimination** – to know the difference between good and bad, right and wrong. This objective is fulfilled by strengthening one's mind power through hearing from scriptures and simultaneously by avoidance from bad elements and bad environment in the society.

2. **Determination** – to apply oneself towards good habits. This is achieved by strengthening oneself with powerful tools like mediation, which will increase the purity in the heart and thus the resistance mechanism increases, which in turn destroys one's inclination towards bad company, things or habits.

Therefore, if we listen to our mind which may pull us to do wrong things, we may get into the zone of bad habits. But when we listen intently to the intelligence, we apply the reasoning effectively and thus avoid bad elements and move forward to cultivating good habits.

One can experience the power of good habits to overcome the inclination to get addicted to bad habits by involving in powerful techniques as given below.

(i) **By Yoga and meditation** – As discussed earlier, both yoga and meditation have a powerful effect on one's subconscious mind. We can take the example of focussing light through a lens. In science, we did experiments on lenses wherein a lens could burn paper or cotton when the focussed lens was on to them. Similarly if we involve in programs like yoga and meditation, which increase our concentration, then naturally it can burn away all impurities in the heart. All impurities in the mind are like viruses in the hard disk. The meditation technique, especially the mantra meditation, scans and destroys all the viruses just like wiping a dusty mirror with a wet cloth. By cleaning the mirror, the mirror shines brightly and naturally we can see our face clearly. Similarly, chanting of a mantra which is approved by the scriptures will surely destroy all the impurities and bad habits within us and gives clear intelligence to cultivate good habits.

(ii) **By studying values based books** – If one cultivates the habit of reading sacred and sanctified books like the Ramayana, the Bhagavad-Gita, the Srimad Bhagavatam, the Bible, the Quran etc, one sharpens his intellect and the wisdom to demarcate and wriggle free from bad elements in the society.

Either yoga and meditation or studying the Holy Scriputres do not stop us from the freedom we have for the addiction towards bad habits. It's a fact that chanting the Holy name of the Lord is a universally accepted and time-tested, non-sectarian method of bringing about the blossoming of consciousness to its highest level of pure love for God and all other living beings. The process of chanting, as prescribed in many sacred scriptures, frees one from selfish motives and desires; on the other hand it provides meaning to life. This act of chanting will enable us to experience everlasting peace and happiness, which is certainly independent of the state of the body and the external factors.

The Native American Indians mentions that all our hearts have two types of dogs: a good dog and a bad dog. Among these two, the bad dog is howling for vengeance along with reckless action for developing bad habits, whereas the good dog is looking for morals, values, ethics, integrity and hankering for the mode of goodness by leading a life centered on good character. And as such there is battle between these two dogs in our hearts. The dog that we feed the most is going to be the stronger between the two. Here, a question may arise on how to feed these dogs. It is by the way we make our choices at every moment in our life and by the values we hold sacred. Both good and bad are embedded within all of us. Nourishing the positive along with goodness and starving the negativity along with the badness in us will result in real advancement in life. If we have the necessary determination and resolve, and if we make the right choices in life, to nourish our divine nature, we are sure to lead a victorious life, thus avoiding the bad habits and simultaneously developing the good ones.

Srikanth: It was certainly a pleasure interacting with you Hari. Thank you very much.

Hari: You're welcome Srikanth, Really it's also a great pleasure talking to you. Thank you.

HOW TO DEAL STRESS

Seated by the side of the Bhadrakali tank, a stone's throw distance from the popular sacred place of Bhadrakali temple in Warangal, Miss Praveena SriRam, a final year student of chemical engineering and general secretary of Value education club of our institute for the academic year 2012-2013, finds solace in the serene locale, far away from the busy roads of the city which are swelled with chaos, smoke and dust. Just by swaying her fingers on the surface of the river water and by looking at the sunset, a sense of satisfaction pervades her heart, something she couldn't find even by solving the most intellectual of problems in engineering mathematics. She's not alone; Saranya and Puja, her classmates and friends, support her reflection in the similar way.

Incidentally, they find one of the faculty members of the institute Dr. P. Hari Krishna visiting the temple along with his family members. These students try to convey their gratitude in arranging a special talk on "Stress management" by Dr. V. Srikanth Reddy, Professor psychology at SVU college of engineering Tirupati just few days back. After that they will start discussing with the faculty member about their doubts on this topic and this chapter presents these discussions between the faculty and his wife with the students. Additionally some more important points are also included for the benefit of the reader of this book.

Praveena: Sir, we are happy to see you and your family members here at this place.

Hari: Yes Praveena. I am also happy to see you also here enjoying nature. By the way she is my wife Dr. K. Hima Bindu, who is working as associate professor in Kakatiya Medical College, Warangal and here are my kids Sri Vaishnavi and Krishna Chandra.

Puja: Sir, do you have some time. We wish to clarify some points on ways of dealing the stress among the student community, in continuation to the expert talk by Prof. V. Srikanth Reddy from Sri Venkateswara University, Tirupati.

Hari: Yes, sure, let us all sit here.

About stress

Praveena: Thank you sir, in today's world, everyone has become busy in their life with everything to be done very fast. This kind of a busy and fast-paced life results in many serious consequences, on the physical and mental health of human beings.

Saranya: I agree. By reviewing the history, one can identify that the human civilization has faced many debilitating diseases like Plague, polio and pneumonia etc. But in the recent days, the human society is getting affected with an unidentified, most dangerous alarming characteristic disease named Stress. This stress factor is observed as one of the most difficult one to eliminate from one's life and it is mainly causing psychosomatic diseases or heart diseases rather than some simple physical ones. It is found to be a major factor that creates disturbances in one's emotional, family and social life in addition to ruining one's entire career.

Puja: Let me add that it is also found that stress diminishes creativity, enthusiasm, commitment, effectiveness of humans and results in creating a general dissatisfaction in the life.

Hari: You are right in your observations. Seated along the banks of a placid reservoir, such a scenic locale does help us channelize our thought process along these lines. Yes! The stress factor has created a great havoc even in the technically advanced countries like the USA, in terms of the number of people who are greatly troubled by this disease. In fact, the research team from the medical college of Cornell University has declared that this stress factor can affect the person both physically and mentally along with leading to several behavioral changes. Due to blind following of western culture by the Indian young generation in recent times, it is noticed that many countries' cultures got warped by modernization and globalization. Hence, this stress mania is spreading rapidly among young generation after the MNC culture has started to pervade here. This results in many ways as physically — heart disease, constant fatigue, stiff neck and back ache, ulcer, indigestion, diarrhea, headache and fatigue — or mentally in the form of lack of concentration, confusion, difficulty in making decisions, forgetfulness, panic attacks etc. Sometimes people affected from this disease are found to get behavioral changes in terms of restlessness, irritable and rage behavior, addiction to smoking, drinking habits and further leading them to take deadly decision like committing suicide.

Saranya: But, is suicide not a sin?

Hari: Yes! In the entire beautiful creation, it is only the most intelligent form of life — the human being — who will think and perform this great sinful act of suicide, thus ending his/her life before the desired period by nature. The peculiarity of this stress factor is that it is uniquely different from what we normally think of as a disease because it does not exhibit any biological structure similar to that of a germ or a virus. Rather than functioning from the lurk in dark sewers or contaminated water, this stress factor results from the regularity of one's life style; in other words, from the mental and physical functioning of one's own self. It's really surprising to note the fact that even though this stress factor or quality of one's entire life is dictated by the state of the mind, one is not concentrating on this issue and is unable to allocate any time for maintaining proper sound psychological mental condition.

Stress in the young age

Praveena: But Sir, this seems to affect us youngsters the most.

Hari: Yes, absolutely; in any person's life, young age also popularly known as teenage is the most critical stage. This is mainly due to the fact that at this age there are changes in the body, of both male and female, because of which many of the young people are caught up in a confused mental state. Of course, the level of changes is more in case of girls than in boys. During this age, people get attracted to the opposite sex and desire to get near them along with wishing to spend time with them.

Bindu: Adolescence is found to be a transition period and for teenagers the idea of joy and enjoyment creep into the minds. Therefore, it is the duty of parents and elders in family to monitor the behavioral changes and guide them in a correct way. This stress factor enters into their life very fast when their problems or anxieties or doubts are not cleared off regularly. To overcome their curiosity in learning more about the physical changes and mental attraction to opposite sex, they approach cheap material on sex and sex education. This action creates more problems to them both immediately and also in the long run. It's an open secret that many young people are visiting psychiatrists now-a-days for different types of psychological problems and many others are not in a position to identify the problem itself and are not willing or ready to solve this great disease. Hence, it is absolute necessity for the present younger generation to understand this stress factor and most possible reasons for avoiding the same by adopting some simple remedial techniques in our lives based on the Holy scriptures so that one can live peacefully and happily.

Importance of Stress

Saranya: Could you elaborate on this concept of stress? To help us understand it better.

Hari: In any branch of engineering this term stress is really an important parameter to analyze and to understand the design of any member. It is generally defined as the internal resistance offered by the body and which is necessary to maintain the equilibrium system in any type of engineering. One may extend the same to human beings as wonder that stress is certainly not a dangerous one; rather it is an essential ingredient for the normal functioning of the humans. The reason being, without stress there would be no life at all! People fail to realize the fact that this stress is very natural phenomenon which develops in our body and is the important part of our life. This type of stress which is extended above analogically (that we are in need of) is called as eustress, but we should not have the same stress for longer time periods which then becomes as distress. The eustress in general helps us to keep alert in our life and simultaneously motivates us to face the troubles and challenges that come in our life to develop the techniques to solve these problems smoothly. Whereas, distress on the other hand, results whenever our body or mind over reacts to certain situations or events of life and sometimes, whenever something happens beyond the paradigm or capacity of the body or mind. And incidentally under such circumstances, the important eustress gets converted to a diseased distress condition.

Bindu: As a doctor, I think I can explain the difference between eustress and distress conditions, by taking the example of our body temperature. The temperature of our body in general is supposed to be around 98.6^0 Fahrenheit and never do we have to bring it to zero. But under some circumstances under which if the temperature goes to more than or less than this normal value, then problems arise. Similarly whenever the stress in our system goes beyond the eustress levels without any control, then it creates problems to our psychological system and slowly reduces the immune power of our body, similar to that of a silent killer.

Hari: Stress can also be due to the result of wear and tear phenomenon, our minds and bodies experience as we attempt to cope with the continually changing environment. And stress is not something that affects us from outside, it is the response given by the survival instinct in our body itself. For example, for the student community, examinations period is considered as the most troublesome and uncomfortable phase of life. Due to high levels of stress that prevail during this period, many students abandon food and sometimes even rest. By analyzing such situations one can understand that the two fundamental needs of every living entity are sustenance and protection.

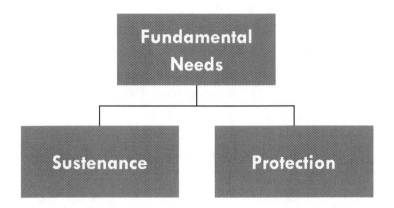

Through sustenance, we take care of the necessities of life like taking food, water, air etc... and from protection, we take shelter from the external environmental conditions like extreme heat, extreme cold, diseases, physical damage to the body, mental afflictions (to the mind), circumstances like failure or death of a dear one etc... that are unfavourable situations to one's mind. In general, by constitution our body has a complex network of systems for arranging extra supply of energy whenever it is forced upon by problematic or troublesome or threatening situations. Hence, this term stress which makes one's life miserable is simply the response of the body system to situations that are perceived by the body as threatening conditions for a happy and comfortable life.

Puja: That was very detailed and scientific.

Causes of Stress

Saranya: Absolutely; coming back, what really are the causes of stress?

Hari: A valid question. Let's analyze the probable causes, which may create this problematic stress especially for students. These causes are generally categorized as physical, mental, environmental, academic and work-related. Let's understand them in detail.

Physical causes: As discussed above, for sustenance of the body we need to have proper food, water and air. But now-a-days people are getting addicted to a type of food which is not good for the physical health. For example taking too much of coffee, tea, smoking, alcohol, drugs etc. can titillate the tongue momentarily and give an artificial sense of elation or relaxation, but actually they increase our stress levels and hence better to avoid. As per scriptures, it is preferable to take natural products like vegetables, fruits, milk, cereals, and sprouts which are nutritious.

Mental causes: Due to the prevailing culture in modern day human society, our mind gets accustomed to a particular set of behavioral patterns like customs and social norms which are derived and established due to great efforts by our grandparents and ancestors. Everyone is comfortable and safe within these approved mental patterns along with the established norms and one may feel threatened and uncomfortable when they are violated. Our survival instinct, classifies each sound, sight and gesture as positive or negative. We get mental stress due to various reasons which could be due to certain type of behavior exhibited by people around us, while working with deadlines or when somebody cheats or insults us etc.

Environmental causes: Although it looks simple, sometimes changes in the environmental conditions like extreme heat or cold, pollution, over-crowded trains or buses also affect us. But the intensity of the effect depends on body resistance or stamina called *prana shakti*. This is the basic reason why different people seem to be affected in different degrees under the same environmental conditions.

Academic related causes: Many young students are affected with academic related stresses because of cut throat competition in studies. In recent times, with eagerness to pursue professional courses like engineering, medicine etc…people are found struggling hard, from as early as eighth standard. And after assiduous attempts to assimilate concepts for many hours every day and qualifying the most competitive of exams. It's just the starting point. After joining, they struggle hard to maintain their academic profile to secure good grades, which in turn is required to get good placements. Such a pursuit demands defying high levels of competition along with a feeling of insecurity at the college level.

Therefore, each student who is doing his professional degree is under high pressure in many ways like

- to meet the expectations of the parents
- to compete with fellow class mates in academic and extra-curricular performance
- to prove himself for his capabilities

Some of the students are facing high levels of stress due to lack of support from family members, either financially or due to broken relationship of their parents. It's not an exaggeration that some of the students in our institute have almost left their studies because of the personal problems like divorcing of parents in recent times.

Saranya (astonished): That's indeed true and sad.

Hari: In addition, incompetence in studies and the unmanaged or poorly managed time during college level also cause lot of stress. Surprisingly, many students face a lot of problems because of the attraction towards the opposite sex along with the desire to impress people – the opposite sex especially, relatives, peers and faculty. They are sometimes forced to spend a lot of time and money for the satisfaction of the lover. And many times they are pressurized to maintain the continuity of relationships and in case of broken love issues, there is no limit for the turmoil they undergo to come back to normal. Now-a-days due to unmitigated exposure to pornography through internet or other sources, students are even forced to indulge in illicit relationships with opposite sex that result in health problems in addition to forced abortions.

Work-related Causes: This is another of the major factors that is troubling the human society, now-a-days especially during their job because of urgency addiction problem. Most of the people who work in giant multinational companies are always fighting with deadlines in their professional life. And some people have the habit of doing any work always at the eleventh hour because of lack of planning of the work or due to their laziness, which leads to tension and stress at the end.

Suicides – the present day stupid idea

Puja: We've seen so many cases of the same, in my friends and relatives. Sadly, in our institute also, some students have committed suicide last year and I've heard from people that when stress reaches a peak, it results in suicide.

Hari: I was just heading to address this nuisance next - the present day stupid idea called as suicide. If we look at the world today, there is a lot to be really depressed about: pollution, feigned relationships people, rudeness exhibited in behaviour rooted in selfishness and egotism and many more others. Such attitude make people weak at heart thereby cropping up thoughts of ending lives by committing suicides for small reasons. One will be surprised to look at some of the statistics of suicides.

Globally over 1 million people commit suicide every year, in other words it means that one death due to this suicide for every 40 seconds. Alarmingly the proportion of people who attempt suicides is about 10 times more than the actual number of deaths; in other words, for every 4 seconds one person is attempting to commit suicide. By the year 2020, it is predicted that the number of suicide attempts along with deaths will be doubled. Even in a country like India, which is supposed to be highly cultured, such cases of suicides are on the rise, mostly in teenage and middle aged people (i.e between the ages of 15 to 35 years). Such a situation is alarming – to become aware that the number of people killing themselves are more than the number of deaths due to wars and murders combined.

World Health Organization (WHO) in collaboration with the International Association for Suicide Prevention observes the tenth of September as the annual world suicide prevention day. The objective is to call forth the attention of people to understand the prevention methods for controlling the idea of committing suicides. According to WHO the various causes for suicides are mental disorders including depression, alcohol and substance abuse, antisocial and offending behaviours, poor socio-economic, educational and social circumstances, poor physical health, stressful events such as relationship breakups, loss of loved ones, breakage in love or sometimes threat to the love between two people, arguments with family members or friends, financial, legal or work-related problems and humiliation. Therefore, the ultimate expression of frustration and hopelessness, wherein one sees on the landscape of life only problems everywhere and solutions nowhere, is the main reason for one to take up such a coward decision to end life prematurely.

How to deal with crises in our lives

Saranya: I truly agree with each and every word of what you've said. In fact, we've read about the same widely in newspapers and magazines. But, we still don't fathom such a behavior. However, how does one deal with such a crisis?

Praveena: Instead of delving deeper into the problem, we would like to hear from you the solution to it. How does one deal with it and overcome?

Hari: In the entire world, every one seeks happiness. But true happiness is a result of inner fulfillment. History clearly indicates that sincere and knowledgeable people have turned towards spirituality to achieve a higher taste of happiness along with quality of life. The general tendency in today's human life style people get trapped by being obsessed with quantitative rather than qualitative values. This attitude is making their mind imprisoned in superficiality. And because of stresses and anxieties they become prisoners of their success.

Real wisdom should be to build a strong foundation so that we can prepare our mind to tolerate the ups and downs in life. As such, life has dualities: happiness-distress, success-failure, honor-dishonor, victory-defeat, pleasure-pain etc. Therefore, when we build a strong internal foundation in life, then whatever ups and downs or rewards and trails that come in our life are opportunities to gain the necessary experience to handle such situations. A really successful person is one who will see an opportunity in every situation of life. For example, a person may see a glass as half filled with water with positive attitude where as for the other it may be half empty.

Let us discuss the interesting story of ostriches when they come upon some crises in their life. When a wild animal like a lion or a tiger comes to feed on the ostrich, the fearful ostrich runs as far as possible and when it cannot run further, it digs a hole in the ground and hides his head in the hole and foolishly thinks that "I am safe now." Similarly, when a fox comes to eat a rabbit, the rabbit closes his eyes and just forgets that the fox is on the hunt. But in reality, the fact is that the lion is going to eat the ostrich and also the fox is going to eat the rabbit. Putting the head into the hole or closing the eyes will not change the situation or solve the problem. Even the humans have the habit of watching serials or sports in televisions to forget problems. It is similar to the attitude of putting head into the ground or closing the eyes to get away from the problem.

A person should perform his duties either as student or as a professional with full power and determination along with a lot of enthusiasm but at the same time he should not get attached to the results. A happy, plain thinking, positive attitude person who is in need of fulfilling life requires the art of controlling his mind rather than being controlled by it. If one can transform greed into generosity, arrogance into humility, envy into appreciation, selfishness into service attitude, despair into hope, he/she sees only opportunities in life.

Puja: Sir, I've heard this cliché — the ability to view the glass as half full and not half empty and the repeatedly used phrase emphasizing on the ability to view every situation in life as a blessing and as an opportunity. But, how does one cultivate tolerance?

Art of Tolerance

Hari: As we grow in the spiritual strength of our minds, we will learn to see the life in a proper perspective — not as a 100m sprint to achieve a short momentary pleasure, but rather as a 100 km marathon to attain everlasting joy and happiness. When flickering material pleasures constitute life goals, the reversals which jeopardize these pleasures can devastate us, creating a situation of nothing to live for. But when our lives have a more enduring and lofty goal — to attain love of God — we can tolerate the adversities, knowing that they cannot stop us from attaining our life's goal. In one Holy Scripture, it is said that "The non-permanent appearance and disappearance of happiness and distress are similar to the appearance and disappearance of winter and summer seasons in a year. They arise from sense perception and one must learn to tolerate them without being disturbed."

As we are living in a world of dualities, it becomes a challenge to adjust one's mind to maintain integrity while tolerating dualities. A coin has two sides – a head and a tail – and when you want the head side of a coin you must also accept automatically the tail side; as they are inseparable. The above statement describes how distress is inseparable from happiness and similarly how success is inseparable from failure. In today's modern world, the root of the problem lies in the mentality that "I want to be in control of destiny either today or tomorrow"; but actually we are not in control. Everyone has to lose beauty, physical capabilities and sometimes money and many other things also. Hence, it is certainly a humble experience to live in this world peacefully because we are not the controllers of any activity or the results of it.

The Vedic texts explain that we can spiritualize our talents and resources by using them in the service of the Lord and also to all the brothers and sisters in His family. When you are engaged in the service of the Lord and His creation, it fills our heart with inner joy and releases us from craving for the external pleasures. When we attempt to love the Lord and try to serve Him, He bestows us with the divine vision to see His loving hand in the reversals or ups and downs in our lives. Just as an intelligent child sees the love of the mother, not only in her encouragement, but also in her chastisement, similarly we can see the Lord's love not only in terms of success but also in times of failure.

The correct understanding that all the reversals in our lives come due to our past misdeeds, as per the impartial law of karma, would ensure that we don't feel victimized or depressed. Rather we feel empowered well aware that we can create a bright future for ourselves by living in harmony of Lord's teachings, no matter how bleak the present situation may be. Even amidst reversals, one can see the road to eternal glory that is beckons us. Whatever failures that come upon our lives they refine us, not define us. Moreover, by knowing the fact that the Lord is not just a neutral judge but a loving father, and by chanting His names along with praying to Him, we become blessed with the inner strength to not only face but emerge stronger and stronger to tolerate sufferings. Therefore, by assuaging our mind about the position of the Lord in our hearts, we can march confidently through all the reversals or ups and downs of our life very smoothly.

One who can tolerate is the Great

Puja: In other words, is that a sign of a man's greatness?

Hari: Very well said. You see, in the entire world, people like to adore great people and also people like to become great in their own way. But one has to understand what greatness actually is. Is greatness comes by possessing wealth or position? Some of the most degraded people in the world are billionaires and occupy high echelons in the society. Some of these people are also supporting terrorism to prevail in the society. Is it greatness? Is greatness a result of attaining fame or by being a good singer or dancer, having a beautiful body, being strong or athletic or being heroic? What is it, actually?

According to the universal principle of all spiritual paths: one's greatness is estimated by one's ability to tolerate provoking situations. This factor should be understood by every individual. This one statement transcends sectarianism. It's easy to make a show of being great, but when challenged or forced to face provoking situations, then comes the actual test for character. Vedic scriptures give us this as a constant theme and to achieve this, one has to start understanding spirituality and its importance in life.

The data that speaks

Let us analyze the data from the findings of eminent people on the importance of having spirituality in increasing the tolerance and avoiding distress in their lives thereby decreasing the potentiality of opting for committing suicides.

Patrick Glynn, the Associate Director of George Washington University reports the empirical findings in his book - 'God' on the importance of spiritual meetings in minimizing the chances of suicides as

(i)   The persons who did not attend any religious meetings were four times more likely to commit suicides rather than those who attend these types of meetings regularly.

(ii) There is absolute negative relationship between religious commitment and suicides.

(iii) Lack of attending any spiritual meetings has been found to be the single best predictor of suicide rates, better even than unemployment.

The American Journal of Epidemiology (March, 2002) reports that the suicide risk among the people aged between 20 to 34 years is 3 to 6 times higher than among non-religious people than the religiously active people. In the similar direction, the studies by West Virginia University in Morgantown which are published in the American Journal of Health Promotion, 2001 show that the spiritual practices like meditation, prayers and chanting of the Holy names of the Lord will result in improved mental health, the lack of which is considered to be the main cause of distress in our lives which further leads to committing suicide.

One eminent spiritualist states that "the act of suicide is violation of nature's law. Nature has provided you a certain type of body to live in it for certain days, and suicide certainly means that you go against the laws of nature, you untimely stop the duration of life." Wisely speaking, the material body we reside in is not ours to destroy it; it is a gift given by nature to help us advance spiritually. When we destroy it prematurely, we become karmic criminals, liable for huge punishment. Hence suicide is a total failure — it doesn't end our problems, rather it aggravates them.

Praveena: In a subject matter so deep, it's so sad that we look at life superficially without giving it any thought. But, if I revert to the earlier discussion as you mentioned, why is it that the most intelligent of species — the human — indulges in an act, as foolish as this?

Why only humans commit suicide?

Hari: Yes, it's indeed surprising that it is only humans in the entire creation who make this foolish choice, as you rightly put. Interestingly, the agony of frustration, which is the cause of suicides, is not unique to humans; even other creatures suffer as a result of their inability to gratify these senses, especially the inability to mate. But no animal, bird or aquatic commits suicide. Joyce Stewart, an animal behaviorist, stated in the Times on March 3rd, 2005 that "I have never heard of any animal taking their own lives by committing suicide."

In the Holy Scriptures, it is described that we as spirit souls occupy various material bodies for enjoying different bodily pleasures. As per the nature of our material desires, we wander through various species of life – human and subhuman, seeking pleasure through food, sex, sleep and show of strength. All these activities offer at best temporary enjoyment, whereas we long for everlasting happiness, which we can find only in eternal love for the Supreme Lord. Consequently, we always feel dissatisfied, irrespective of the body we live in. The present human body is special for all of us as it offers the required consciousness to have ultimate emotional fulfillment that comes from loving the Lord. This supreme spiritual joy that is available to us as humans far exceeds any pleasure that is possible in any other species. However, at the same time, this human consciousness that brings the ultimate ecstasy also make us prone to suffering far more than animals if we choose to love anyone other than the Lord.

When animals love, they enjoy finite physical and mental pleasure – as per their level of consciousness. When they lose a mate, they experience corresponding finite suffering; and they just find another mate and go on with the life. But as humans when we love another person, we are anticipating through that love the same unlimited ecstasy which comes from loving the Lord. So when our love fails, our suffering is also unlimited. The more we invest our love in attempted substitute for the Lord; even more shattering will be our dreams which agonize us; ultimately to the point where we may want to end our very life. We've got this special human form of life after many non-human lives and surely this life is meant for a special purpose of developing love for God. So, in one sense, by accepting the materialistic conception of life, all of us are committing spiritual suicide because we are destroying our soul's prospects for a blissful spiritual life.

Right choice

In nature, a tree will stand in the scorching sun to give shade to other living beings and it will bear the freezing cold of the winter; further, it supplies wood to create heat for all of us. And needless to say, it will silently give up its life to share its body to build a house for others to stay comfortably. This is real tolerance. To become great, one should develop this attitude of being more tolerant than a tree. This may seem impossible, but it is actually our true inner nature. When a person develops spiritual and true love towards all, there is unlimited tolerance and humility.

There will be many temptations and provoking situations that will come upon us in our lives. The important question for all of us to contemplate upon is what we value as sacred in our lives. Our principle should be to be a first class human being, and we should live with integrity, character, morality and ethics. As we discussed previously, real happiness is a result of inner fulfillment, which is attained when one's life principles and life are in harmony with the nature. The greatest necessity in today's human society is to be the good example and the best example is one who lives with dignity and impeccable character. Now-a-days, we seldom find people with such qualities. If we want to generate such great qualities like ethics, character and integrity to make a sustainable foundation so that we can weather any storm in life, we must cultivate spiritual realization.

Praveena: So, am I right to conclude that spirituality should become an integral part of educational system, so that the foundation on which one's life principles are built is strong?

A call for action on solutions

Hari: Yes, very much; to tackle the problems of stress or of suicide, we need more education in terms of stress management, positive thinking, workshops and importantly psychiatric counseling. These types of efforts will surely help curb high levels of stress under crying situations and assist in taking intelligent decisions under critical circumstances. And to become a tolerant person, one should re-harmonize one's life style with intrinsic spiritual education and one should learn the art of loving God. Such an education comes to the help of those distressed considering suicide by helping view material problems as wake up calls to reclaim the right for a meaningful and joyful spiritual life. A great scholar once remarked that it is only when the night gets dark that the stars shine through brightly.

Therefore, we have to understand that the current darkening of our material behavior is what we are in need of to observe the stars of eternal spiritual truths that illuminate our lives.

After understanding the definition and causes for this great epidemic "Stress" upon the entire humanity in general and student community in particular, let us now intelligently think of finding a remedial method to this problem of stress. It would be worthwhile to sit and contemplate for a few minutes, the meaning and purpose of our life for which we are working so hard, stressing our bodies and minds. If we would not devote this time, we would be like that plane which took off well and is traveling with a good speed, but not knowing where it is going. Many of the psychiatrists unanimously recommend having proper life style to get the solution for every situation in our lives.

Saranya: It has so far been an enlightening discussion. We've just learned so much, unaware of the passage of time. Taking it forward, can you suggest practical solutions that we can apply in our day-to-day life?

Practical solutions for youth

Hari: This is the most important part of the discussion. How well we can learn from our mistake and address them effectively. The possible solutions to avoid stress in youth are:

1. By having regulated life style
2. By balancing academics with harmless recreation
3. By focusing on positive strengths rather than negative habits
4. By suitably managing most valuable time
5. By associating with like-minded friends whose company will help cultivate values, good habits and success in academics
6. By regularly studying wisdom inducing literature on value based education. Such an endeavor helps elevate one's outlook of life by imbibing strength to face any nerve-racking situation, be it broken love, broken relationship with family members, academic competition or failures in life.

Lifestyle management

Stephen Covey, in his famous book, 'Seven habits of highly effective people', indicates that happiness is possible only when the following four needs are properly met with. Lack of it, he says, would surely make one feel empty and incomplete.

- The need to live is our PHYSICAL QUOTIENT (PQ); such as diet, exercise and relaxation.
- The need to love is our SOCIAL QUOTIENT (EQ); the need to love and to be loved.
- The need to learn is our INTELLECTUAL QUOTIENT (IQ); the need to develop and grow.
- The need to leave a legacy is our SPIRITUAL QUOTIENT (SQ); the need to understand the purpose to life

Each of these needs is vitally important and when even one of them is not fulfilled, it reduces the quality of life. If you're in debt or poor health, don't have adequate food, clothing and shelter, if you feel alienated and alone, mentally stagnant, lack a sense of purpose and integrity, quality of life suffers. Certain factors like vibrant health, economic security, richness, satisfying relationships and ongoing personal and professional development along with a deep sense of purpose contribute to creating quality of life. These needs are real, deep and interrelated. The problems in life come when we sow one thing expecting to reap something entirely different.

Physical Needs (PQ): The vibrant health of a person is based on natural principles. It grows over time as a result of regular exercise, balanced diet, sound mind-set, avoiding substances that are harmful to the body and adequate rest. Rather than paying the correct price, we are caught up in the illusion of our appearance – clothes, makeup, quick-fix weight-loss programs (actually proven to contribute to long-term problems instead). It's an empty promise. It brings about flickering pleasures and is cotton candy. There's no substance in it. It doesn't last. Mere bathing of the body is not maintenance, alike mere dusting of a scooter. If we don't take care of the body, we can never be free from the ill effects of negative stress that always keep afflicting us. Your slogan should be: 'I shall stay healthy.' Only a healthy body can continuously fight. Efforts to remain healthy keeps you fit and also to wriggle free from the vicious cycle of stress. In order to accomplish this, correct your lifestyle. The three components of life to make a person healthy are balanced diet, necessary exercise and very importantly suitable relaxation.

Social Needs (EQ): Quality relationships are built on certain principles like the principle of trust, which grows out of trustworthiness, the character to make and keep commitments, sharing of resources, being caring and responsible, loving unconditionally etc. It is easier to get a fix of love than to work on being a loving person.

Intellectual Needs (IQ): We often go for the illusion of 'cramming' instead of long-term development and growth. We're into 'getting the degree, then getting the job so that you can get the money, so you can buy the things and therefore you'll be successful.' But what does that kind of 'successes' bring? An intelligent person should first realize what is really important in life and what type of activities will bring real success.

Spiritual Needs (SQ): Our life has to have a vision, mission, and purpose — why and for whom are we living? What do I value in life? Is it Money, Family, Friends, Position, Prestige? What do I want to get out of my life? While one should lead a life of balance between job and home, work and entertainment, one should also inquire into spirituality for a long-term higher purpose of life itself. **Be natural; it is natural for you to love and serve God!**

In our natural state, we genuinely live happily. A fish doesn't struggle to swim, he swims; a bird doesn't struggle to fly, he flies; a cuckoo doesn't struggle to sing, she sings. Similarly if we can understand our true nature — to love and to serve — and bring out that innate quality into our lives, it would make a remarkable difference. People who lead selfish lives don't truly experience life as much as one that lives a God-centered self-less life for the sake of others. There is enormous, valuable information available for modern man in the wisdom-rich literature: The Ramayana, The Mahabharata, The Bhagavad-Gita, The Bible and The Quran. Fundamental values in life should be sound, based on these teachings of the above works so that one leads a stress-free life.

Saranya: This is universal, beyond sectarian themes. But, to cultivate such a life and thus inculcating the resolve to manage stress is mountainous, not easy. Is it not?

Learn to manage the Stress

Hari: You can make your Mind, a Friend or Enemy. The Master Mind dictates and the servile senses follow. The nature of the mind is flickering and unsteady. The yoga system is meant to control the mind in such a way that the mind will act as your friend. Sometimes, the mind acts as a good friend and during some other times it acts as an enemy. As we are part and parcel of the Supreme God, who has infinite independence, we also have minute or finite independence. It is the mind which is controlling that independence; therefore the mind may take us either to a spiritual place like a temple, church, mosque or to a nightclub. The mind is a friend when it is under the control of the intelligence and makes life serene, self-controlled, simple, pure and stress-free. The mind becomes an enemy when we allow ourselves to be tamed by its desires and that of the sense objects; then it becomes uncontrollable from within. Therefore as a learned human being, one should learn managing stress under uncontrollable circumstances.

Saranya: Thank you very much Sir. It certainly was enlightening.

Puja: I'm sure assimilation and implementation of this wisdom will take us places and provide us with the happiness that we eternally seek.

Praveena: I'm convinced that the solace I seek in this serene place is an infinitesimal portion what I shall experience when I serve the Lord wholeheartedly.

Hari: Wonderful! It was my pleasure discussing this subject with you all. Hope you will remember all these discussions and be able to deal this great disease of stress effectively in your entire life. May the supreme god bless you all.

Bindu: Wish you all the best

TIME MANAGEMENT

Rajeev, a final year student of our institute, has been finding his life the going tough in terms of balancing time for college studies, training and placement section preparations in addition to normal academic examinations, along with family issues and spiritual life. During a visit to one of the faculty, he managed to get his doubts clarified by Dr. P. Hari Krishna.

Rajeev: Good morning Sir. Hope I am not disturbing you.

Hari: Hai Rajeev, a very good morning. How are you? You are most welcome. I am just completing my preparation to the next class in the afternoon.

Rajeev: Sir, if you are free for some time, I wish to enquire with you about some of my doubts regarding my time scheduling. Now-a-days, I find management of time for my daily activities is becoming very challenging. Hence, I would like to get certain doubts clarified in this direction so that I can better manage it.

Hari: Sure. Please let me know how I may help you.

Rajeev: Sir, what is time management? And how does one go about it, practically.

Hari: Time management is simply defined as the person's ability to keep balance between daily activities effectively by properly prioritizing the importance of activities. It requires both discipline and flexibility to mould to circumstances. Being humans, time management is very important and when one is young, it becomes challenging. For the students especially in the modern day, there are many important things and it becomes essential for them to properly prioritize the most important and urgent ones, so that one can be a successful student, academically and behaviourally.

Rajeev: Ok. I agree with you when you say that it's challenging when one is young. I truly endorse your viewpoint but do you think it's important for us at this age?

Hari: This subject matter 'Time' is very important to be understood; especially by youth. One may look at the clock and announce time at that instant with a superficial conception, but one is not able to recognize the power of time. An old man and a young boy may both look at the same clock, but they see it differently. In case of an old man, he may be apprehensive and also nervous as he sees the clock ticking away fastly. But a young boy, may be impatient and may be wondering why it is not speeding up so that he will grow fast to enjoy life. Contrastingly, old man may stop the clock physically but the time does not stop there. Similarly, young boy may speed up the clock but time doesn't change according to his requirement.

Acronym of Time

This concept of time management is tricky and trendy. In case of student life, this time is the most precious for one who wants to excel with good academics. We can have a simple acronym for the word T.I.M.E. which will help the students to keep them on the correct path always.

T – Task related: Ask yourself in terms of the necessity of doing any activity in life. Because every activity of our life should have a goal and we should not waste our time on unnecessary things.

I – Interest creating: Every effort we put for doing any activity requires interest in completing it. The interest in completing the lab records, assignments, attaining good ranks in examinations, getting a good job in a dream company will make the person effective and efficient to achieve the goal.

M – Managing: Management is the most important part of student life. As a student one has to concentrate on academics, extracurricular activities along with dealing friends and parties etc. Therefore one should be efficient to manage many good and bad people around him so that he can successfully complete all activities in his student life.

E – Education related: Any activity we render during student life should be helpful to our education. Education does not tantamount to just pursuit of a degree but it is actually the process which deals with acquisition, cultivation and dissemination of knowledge. The ultimate goal of education is not to secure employment or a better position in any company, but to make students as good humans with a proper character and life style.

Rajeev: That's an interesting acronym. But, how important is time for one to succeed?

Hari: Good question. In fact, the one important characteristic which distinguishes successful students from unsuccessful ones is their attitude towards time. Generally, successful people consider time as an important resource which should not be wasted but be effectively 'invested'. This type of attitude which is ingrained in their minds makes them realize the value of time. People who recognize the importance of time will do what is required of them to do. They do not mistake being 'active' as being 'busy' and they distinguish between 'important' and 'urgent' matters in life. They are clear about their life time goals and whatever they do in their everyday life is towards accomplishing those goals. They have time for everything which is important in their life. They are relaxed and never tense; most importantly they spend every minute of their time pleasantly, fully enjoying it. They are branded as well 'organized' people by the society. In common, humans perceive time as more valuable than money for its utility, as a resource to be managed so as to get things done.

What happens to those who do not know how to manage their time?

Rajeev: But, what happens to those who do not know how to manage their time?

Hari: Well, let me list them down in points.

- They lose temper to excel in academics
- They collapse mentally and suffer emotionally because of lack of interest in the life
- They miss opportunities because of disorganisation of things
- They accomplish very little of what they actually wanted to do
- They do things haphazardly with no prior planning which leads to reduced efficiency
- They overload themselves, forgetting physical health, mental peace and relationships

Why do we need to learn about Time Management?

Rajeev: My God! I can very well relate to it. On the positive side, why do we actually learn time management?

Hari: Again, let me list them down in points.

- To aim for important life achievements
- To complete academic deadlines efficiently
- To effectively utilise the God-given time for the benefit of oneself and that of others.
- To organise our life properly interms of family, professional and social life
- To accomplish the short-term and long-term goals at the right time
- To not waste our time and other's time
- To learn the art of working smarter rather than harder
- To learn to manage our life without getting unnecessarily frustrated

Rajeev: Sir, That's nice to hear. Do the Vedic scriptures describe the importance of time?

Hari: Definitely! In the Mahabharata, the importance of time is mentioned as follows

Time runs like a wheel
Time is always awake when all other things sleep
Time stands straight upwards when all things fall
Time shuts in all and will not be shut
Time is, was and shall be there always
Time's children be witness for all this and be stable in their lives

Problems are caused by chaos — the lack of order in our life

Also, let me add that traditional time management suggests that problems are caused by chaos — the lack of order in life. By doing things efficiently you will eventually gain control of your life and that increased planning will bring peace and fulfilment that you're looking for.

Organizing can be of three types:

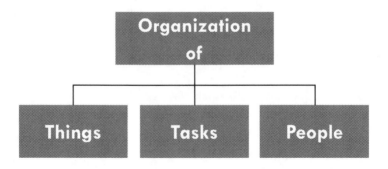

Organization of Things - Creating order for everything from keys, computer, space, filing etc.

Organisation of Tasks - Giving priorities to "to do" using tools from lists to planning charts.

Organisation of People - Defining what you can do and what others can do and delegating.

Rajeev: This reminds me of an approach 'get organized' and I remember reading Stephen Covey having an opinion on this.

Hari: Yes! This 'get organized' approach may save time and lead to clarity, order and higher efficiency. It involves tremendous amount of time to be spent in organizing than producing. Many people think they are getting things accomplished because they are busy organizing when in reality they may be procrastinating and not completing important work. Applied in excess, what is thought as the strength of an organization becomes its own weakness. We can become over structured, inflexible and mechanical. This holds true for organizations as well as individuals; for students, it is very important to understand.

Coming to your question, yes, Stephen Covey, author of the seven habits of highly effective people, disagrees with the above approach. We can control our choice of action but we cannot control the consequences of our choices. The principle-centred leadership approach transcends the traditional prescriptions of being faster, harder and smarter along with many more. Rather than offering another clock, this new approach provides one with a compass; because more important than how fast you are going is to know the destination where you're going.

Various Time Management Techniques for Students

Rajeev: Coming to the practical side of life, can you suggest some time management techniques especially for students?

Hari: Why not! There are many useful techniques which when properly understood and implemented greatly helps the students.

a. Investing time where maximum returns can be achieved
b. Learn to avoid wasting of time.
c. Always being Time conscious and using it wisely.
d. Knowing your type and keeping yourself healthy.
e. Trying to prioritize the activities of your life
f. Learning to delegate works appropriately while you are working in a group.

a. Invest Time where maximum returns can be achieved:

An illustration: Have you ever seen a washer man washing a shirt or pant? Is it necessary to rub the whole shirt with the same pressure? No, need not. The right way should be to give more attention to only those parts of a shirt which tend to get dirtier than others: say, the collar, the lower ends of the arms and the portion near the pockets. Similarly, in our life also, we should invest our time appropriately to get maximum returns with less effort as is explained in the following figure.

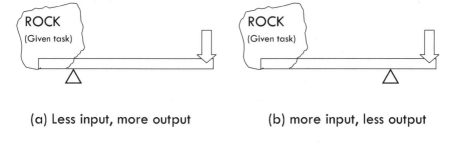

(a) Less input, more output   (b) more input, less output

INTELLIGENCE (MANAGER)   WASTE OF ENERGY (PRODUCER)

From these figures, we can observe that a producer can invest one hour of effort and may produce one unit of results. On the other hand, a manager can also invest one hour of effort and may produce ten or fifty or a hundred units of results through effective delegation. Therefore, management is essentially moving the fulcrum over, and getting maximum output from the minimum input for the system.

b. Learn to Avoid Wasting of Time

- Doing those things that need not be done at all
- Doing certain things that could be and should be done by someone else
- Learning the art of saying 'No' to many activities which will result in wastage of time

c. Always being Time conscious and using time wisely

A school or college is an amazing place where there is always some amusing activity with lot of fun going on. Many times students want to attend those types of programs without fail. But at the same time, if tomorrow you have to submit an assignment or a laboratory record, then one should be careful enough to decide whether to attend such a program or not. In general as academics are the most important for students, we should complete the academics part first before making plans to attend such programs.

d. Knowing your type and keeping yourself healthy

Every human is different in nature and so we have to have our own way of doing things in life. One should not compare oneself with fellow roommates or class mates. As we generally see one may be very intelligent in understanding and remembering and the other may not be that intelligent but still he is hard working. A hard working student may be forced to sit for an hour to complete one assignment whereas an intelligent one may complete the same in half an hour. Therefore, no one should waste his time by comparing with others and later blaming time for not being sufficient to complete the task.

Similarly the health of a student is also very important. One should properly prioritize in terms of eating, sleeping and if possible, for some exercises. In addition to eating healthy food at all times of the day, properly sleeping for the required number of hours one should think of doing some exercises everyday to keep his body healthy. Practicing such a careful life style can make you go for a long way in your successful student life.

e. Trying to prioritize the activities of your life

In our daily life, reversals do happen frequently although we carefully plan many things. Just for example, we may fall sick, or we may lose our laptop or mobile phone etc. Some times you are forced to participate in a dance or drama because of your classmate or close friend in emergency. Therefore, as students, we may have to prioritize, reprioritize and some times reprioritize again and again as things keep changing in life. A person with good management skills will deal with situations effectively without finding a great crisis in his life.

f. Learning to delegate while you are working in a group.

Many a times it happens in student life when you are supposed to complete certain activities as a group. For example doing the project work in a semester or conducting the college day festival, this will be naturally done as group. And when doing certain activities in a group one should be intelligent enough to allocate or delegate certain type of works for all group members. Sometimes, people who want to perform activities on their own for the sake of perfectness will extend themselves to be engaged in all the activities. This creates complex and difficult situations in managing oneself with time. Therefore team work is very important in completing such activities successfully in professional life.

Time Management Matrix

Also, let me share with you something called as the **Time Management Matrix.** This when seen in a structured manner will surely help you understand it systematically.

The two factors that define an activity are:

(1) urgent and
(2) important

Urgent means it requires immediate attention. It's 'now!' Urgent things act on us; for example a ringing phone is urgent. Most people can't stand the thought of just allowing the phone to ring. In our life, urgent matters are usually visible; they press on us and insist on action. They are often pleasant, easy to do. But so often they are unimportant!

Importance on the other hand, has to do with results. If something is important in your life, it contributes to your mission, values, and for the high priority goals. In general, we react immediately to urgent matters. Important matters that are not urgent require more initiative, more proactivity and we must act to seize opportunity, to make things happen. If we don't begin with the end in mind, we don't have a clear idea of what is important, and then we are easily diverted into responding to the urgent.

Let us analyze the urgent and important activities of youth in the form of a matrix.

Time Management Matrix

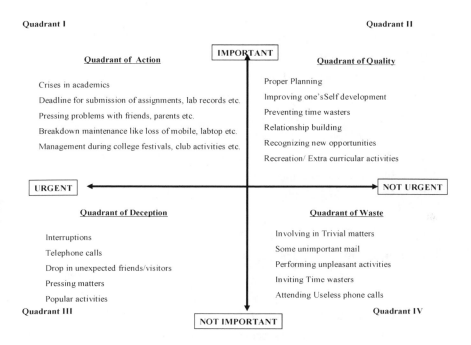

Quadrant I   Quadrant II

IMPORTANT

Quadrant of Action   **Quadrant of Quality**

Crises in academics   Proper Planning

Deadline for submission of assignments, lab records etc.   Improving one's Self development

Pressing problems with friends, parents etc.   Preventing time wasters

Breakdown maintenance like loss of mobile, labtop etc.   Relationship building

Management during college festivals, club activities etc.   Recognizing new opportunities

                                                             Recreation/ Extra curricular activities

URGENT ◄──► NOT URGENT

Quadrant of Deception   **Quadrant of Waste**

Interruptions   Involving in Trivial matters

Telephone calls   Some unimportant mail

Drop in unexpected friends/visitors   Performing unpleasant activities

Pressing matters   Inviting Time wasters

Popular activities   Attending Useless phone calls

Quadrant III   Quadrant IV

NOT IMPORTANT

Am I active or busy? Am I productively busy or unproductively active? Or do I want to be seen as busy by others? Many are unproductively busy due to no proper planning or setting goals or not delegating or being organized. Successful students are not activity oriented; but result oriented. They do not mistake being 'active' as being 'busy'. They distinguish between 'important' and 'urgent'. They are clear about their life time goals. Whatever they do in their life is towards accomplishing these goals. Since they are relaxed and never tense, they manage time for everything effectively. They spend every minute of their time pleasantly, fully enjoying it.

List of Time Wasters

Rajeev: That was so elaborate, easy to refer and understand and most importantly, easily applied in life. Most students get stuck in quadrant 3 or 4. Could you throw more light on it?

Hari: You're right. It's important to identify where one is going wrong. I'll share a list of time wasters that lead to Quadrant III or IV.

* Never setting goals or setting goals and not sticking to them
* Moving around and socializing too much
* Low level of concentration, getting easily distracted by trivial things
* Trying to do more than one thing at a time
* Getting involved in everything
* Making too many personal phone calls regularly
* Not doing the most important academic work at the right time
* Indecisive and postponing decisions
* Liking to help others more than required or to feel important about oneself
* Fear of hurting people or to say 'No'
* Not able to get rid of friends quickly
* Inability to delegate certain works for others during team work activities
* Thinking, "no one else can manage my work if I am absent"
* Forgetting things or badly organized or messy environment, unclean desk
* Looking for too much of perfection in rendering things leading to micromanagement
* Forgetting things and not filing important information to get that in time when required

Students who spend time almost exclusively in Quadrants III or IV basically lead irresponsible lives. Effective people stay out of these two Quadrants because, urgent or not, they aren't important. They may also shrink the Quadrant I to the possible level by spending more time in the Quadrant II.

Time will devour everything

Rajeev: Yes Sir, you have now made me differentiate. Thank you. But, what intrigues me is why youth finds it difficult to understand the power of time.

Hari: The present young generation may find it difficult to understand the power of time in devouring every living entity within this material world. The young people will always look up to the future for more opportunities and do not look into the past. During the childhood, people look forward for vacations so that they can play nicely and during youth they may look forward to complete their graduation early so that they can take up nice career and later get a good spouse to live happily. But due to time factor when the people grow old they become very much inclined to look back, into the past about their good olden days. The aged people, who are mature, observe that those types of expectations and mysteries are longer there, and instead they will forecast that the terminating factor of their lives is coming very fast in terms of death.

If we concentrate on the history, which is in one sense the subject matter of dead people, we find some of them were great, some were bad and insignificant, some people did wonderful things and some did horrible things but everyone got washed away by the waves of time. Time is such a powerful tool that brings every living entity to equal position after their designed life period. We may designate or divide the society based on caste, religion or may be on economical considerations. But after this phenomenon of death, everyone becomes equal – only difference may be that one may be buried into the ground with or with out a memorial and the other may get burnt in fire. And in general, after any disaster municipal people will burn away all the dead bodies which may be of any community. In general, whenever people are bored in their life style, they wish to kill time by one way or other but in reality time only kills everyone in due course without any discrimination.

Time is irrecoverable and unstorable

Rajeev: You just talked about great people. What do they say about time?

Hari: Yes! The great diplomat Chanakya Pandita says that one moment of time is more valuable than wealth equivalent to millions of gold coins. This is easy to understand; if wealth is lost it can be regained, whereas if time is lost it can never be regained as it is irrecoverable. Time is not only irrecoverable, but also not storable. We can choose whether to spend our wealth or not; but we don't have such an option whether to spend time or not; with the passing of every moment, it is automatically and unavoidably being spent. All that we can choose about time is how to spend it. As long as we are in the present material world, time always remains irrecoverable and not storable. That's why we need to be extremely meticulous in investing our time properly. And our greatest time-waster is our own mind. By guarding and investing our time properly, we can safely attain life's supreme destination in the least possible time.

A wise look about time management

Rajeev: Scriptural references best convince me. So, could you highlight on how does a spiritual understanding of time helps in best management of time?

Hari: A wise person with a spiritual back ground observes time with a deep appreciation and values it not only for its utilitarian worth, but also for its intrinsic worth. The fundamental principle of the scriptures is that the soul is beyond time. The body which is occupied by this soul is always changing – from childhood to youth to old age – but the soul remains the same. For the soul there is no birth or death. In other words, it is eternal.

From the spiritual perspective, the present moments of time are very important and should be recognized as it is all that we have. It offers us two types of insights into understanding the present as given below.

- **Time is divine**: It declares that time is a manifestation of God. This type of understanding spiritualizes our vision of time management; we value time not because it gives us the opportunity to do many things, but because it is God himself is offering us that opportunity to do these things.
- **Every moment is precious**: Life at the material level usually reserves importance for certain moments – for example like the moments on the cricket field for cricketers; the moments in the exam hall for students; the moments in the interview room for job seekers. Most other moments usually become mere run-ups for those big make-or-break moments. In our life, certain moments may be more important for our services

externally, but every moment is equally important internally also. Each moment is a precious opportunity to remember God and move closer to him in our own hearts.

Pearls of Wisdom for Effective Time Management

Also, there are certain pearls of wisdom for effective time management

1. If you take care of minutes, hours will take care of themselves.
2. Energy follows Intent. Clearly visualize Goals. Paste it in front of you. Act on it.
3. Think one thing at a time. Don't mess up things and ideas. Don't get into useless dreams.
4. Don't postpone things. Avoid unnecessary delay in academic activities so that you can avoid losing your grades.
5. Don't bite more than you can chew. Evaluate your capacity and resources so that you can involve or participate in any activity.
6. All Entertainment and no academics make anyone a useless student. Don't forget your purpose of coming to college.
7. A person who aims high should be afraid of laziness and popularity. – Emerson
8. Today's speed is beyond financial gains and human values. Follow nature and do things in time.
9. Mind your own business. Share plans, feelings, emotions within a certain limit.
10. Conquer bad mood and boredom through Music, Literature and Arts.
11. Beware of the Time-Sucker One-eyed Monster i.e. Television/ Internet.
12. Avoid unnecessary unhealthy competition. Don't do tasks to show off out of jealousy.
13. Communicate effectively. Remove obstacles and establish Dialogue with tough nuts.
14. Knowledge saves time and trouble.
15. First things first. Do not waste your time in little tasks. Delegate as much as possible.
16. Don't waste time in proving the other person wrong. Utilize it in healthy conversation.

17. Conquer worries & save Time. In general 40% of worries don't happen and for 30% of worries things can't change.
18. Don't waste time in clarifying and justifying mistakes committed. Use the lesson learnt.
19. Give up ego problem to get along with people of different behavioural types. You need them at different levels.
20. Pray to God for help. Prayer gives you Power, Potential, Patience, Support and very importantly the inner strength.

Practical time schedule of students

Rajeev: This was real wisdom. Thank you very much. One last question if I'm not taking too much of your time. Can you throw light on a practical time schedule for students that you think go waste?

Hari: This is a good question because sometimes, students do not know how they will waste their time because of improper time schedule. They may waste their precious time in gossipping, watching TV, sleeping etc. To give a small indication the typical time schedule or a day spent by some of the students on a working day and on a holiday are given below.

On week (college working) days

07.30	Woke up due to alarm, oh! What a nasty dream. Need to go for class at 8 am.
07.40	Had breaker, god! Haven't brushed my teeth today also
08.00 to 12.00	College
12.30 to 13.30	Lunch and gossiping
14.00 to 17.00	College
17.00 to 18.00	Tea at canteen
18.00 to 24.00	Gossipping/ Completing the class work assignments, laboratory records / dinner/ watching movies etc.
24.00	Good night

On Holidays

10.00	Woke up, oh! What a nasty dream
10.30	Had some breaker.
11.00	Didn't miss any of the TV programs
12.00	Bad grub, should eat out at some place on Sundays
13.00	Chatting with friends: couldn't quite come to a decision whether Amir Khan is good enough to replace Salman Khan in a particular film.
13.30	Siesta time
16.30	Tea and game of cards.
1.30	Watching movies.
19.30	Dinner, not quite sumptuous, the gravy was overly salted.
20.00	Remaining part of feature film
21.00	Chatting with friends
22.00	Completed last weeks assignments.
23.00	Had chai and parathas at dhaba.
24.00	Good night, sweet dreams.

The above time schedule both on college working days and holidays gives a picture of how the average student will spend his time. From this we can observe although he is able to allocate only some time for studies, he is wasting most of his valuable time, approximately 4 to 5 hours on working days and about 10 hours on holidays in gossiping/ entertainment etc. If any student who wishes to excel in his studies and career can avoid some of the time wasters like gossiping/ chatting/ talking over phone for longer periods/ going out frequently for food etc he can save at least 40 hours per week which he can efficiently use for academics/ personality development. By such an endeavour surely he can perform better in his academics and can score good grades and further can perform well in Training and placement season to get a lucrative job also. Let me add some of the major benefits of time management.

Major Benefits of Time Management

By saving time and utilizing it effectively a student can achieve many major benefits like:

- Studying well brings success in getting good scores.
- Planning more thoroughly his daily, weekly, monthly and semester schedule
- Avoiding any chance for the crisis
- Creating new ideas/starting new projects.
- Developing your skills for work while you work and play while you play
- Taking care of one self.

Rajeev: Thank you very much sir. It's been a learning experience, the last one hour. I really hope to apply all that you have said. I'll take leave now.

Hari: It's my pleasure Rajeev. I am also really happy to have such wonderful discussions with you on the most important topic of "Time management". Please apply these things in your life and become a nice gentleman and successful professional in the society. Bye. May god bless you.

SELF EMPOWERMENT

India is well known for its Vedic wisdom and used to have well knowledgeable scholars along with a sound academic community and good number of highly creative spiritual scientists, who used to manage their lifestyle interms of good character and regulated behaviour. The entire educational procedure used to have a special inclination towards the more theoretical aspects of science and still used to maintain a good link towards the ancient Indian culture. But now-a-days, the modern educational system is unable to manage the present generation especially during their youth, in terms of maintaining proper character, emotions and relationships. The present day modern scientists are unable to either understand or reveal about who or what the self is. Because the modern society is neglecting or rejecting the spiritual dimension of our lives, the more trouble we have to face in understanding this important factor of "ourself". This can be evident from the present day health problems interms of mental diseases.

Suicide Factor

World Health Organisation (WHO) has declared that in the technologically advanced 21st century, the greatest health hazard is because of the mental diseases like stress, depression, addiction and psychosomatic problems. Based on statistics, this organisation found that every year more than one million people are committing suicide; in other words, atleast one person dying for every 40 seconds. Also more than 10 to 20 times of people are attempting to commit suicide every year, which comes to one attempt in every three seconds. By the year 2020, the prediction says that there will be atleast one person committing suicide for every 20 seconds.

Till the recent times, the suicide factor used to predominate in the elderly group of people, but now-a-days, the suicide phenomenon is predominating in the younger generation also. The World Health Organisation in collaboration with the International Association for suicide prevention observes September 10th of every year as annual world suicide prevention day, to highlight the ways and means to prevent this type of premature and unnecessary deaths. The annual total of more than one million people who are committing suicide is more than the total annual deaths from the wars and crimes put together. Its really a strange and alarming situation in the present day human society that more number of people are killing themselves than killed by others. One should be more concern or cautious to check such a mass killer who is devastating the human psychology.

Why to commit suicide?

Mental diseases and suicides have many causes, but the common and main factor for such a horrible act is frustration in achieving one's goals. When this frustration rises to such an acute level, one feels his very existence to be an agony and then ending of one's existence appears to be the only solution in that circumstance. Its really surprising and horrible to believe that in the entire nature, it is only the humans who are the most intelligent and technically more advanced living beings who commit suicide. WHO has declared suicide as "a tragic social health problem" and further states that there is no proven cure for such a problem. If one tries to understand this problem, then one can realize that due to goals the society sets being incompatible with ourselves, they are inviting frustration in their lives that is leading to many mental health problems and ultimately towards suicide.

To understand the power of our senses, let us take an example of the tongue of our body — which has no bones but it can break the bones of a person if not managed properly. Whenever, the information slips through our tongue in the wrong place, at the wrong time and in front of the wrong person then surely one cannot avoid the consequences that arise due to the mistake of this tongue. This is the difficulty in managing one small part of our human body.

Self Management

At this juncture, one should ask a question like if I am not able to take the responsibility of controlling or managing my own sense organs, how can I take up the responsibility of controlling or managing my life, my family or my workplace and maintain a balance in all the different areas of my life? Through "Self Management" one can learn the art of managing one's own selves along with providing the maturity when to manage, when not to manage, where to manage, how to manage, to what extent to manage and in which way we have to manage. If we do not have the maturity or understanding then it would be difficult to survive as we can easily become victims for own senses. Martin Luther King in his book "From Strength to Love", states that "the means by which we live have outdistanced the ends for which we live". He also further cautioned the entire humanity saying that "we have guided missiles but misguided men"

Now — a — days we find even the most learned and educated are deceived and overpowered by forces like anger, lust, pride, greed, envy and illusion. But, the original nature of the soul is that of peace, love, happiness, purity, wisdom and eternity. One who knows the knowledge of soul, God and the eternal loving relationship between them, can never be bewildered by the pushing's and pulling's of mind and senses.

Hari Krishna Padavala

Importance of Self Management

To understand the importance, we can take a practical life example of an incident from the life of great philosopher 'Socrates'. This great person used to have many philosophical discussions with his friends for hours together in his house, but his wife used to be against such type of discussions. On one such occasion, his wife shouted at him at the top of her voice in front of all his friends saying that they are wasting their valuable time and causing nuisance to her. But, Socrates continued the discussions with his friends with a cool mind but at the same time he could observe that his fellow mates are getting disturbed due to the rash behavior of his wife. He then thought of taking them to a nearby park to continue their discussions. Every one agreed to his suggestion and just as soon as they are about to come out of the house, all of a sudden there was a downpour of water from the first floor on the head and body of Socrates by his wife. All the people were stunned to notice the anger of Socrates wife but Socrates smiled coolly and exclaimed saying, "Friends, previously it was thundering and now it's raining. That's all!" That's how he used to manage his lifestyle without getting disturbed unnecessarily for any incident in his life. Socrates was not only a cool headed gentleman, but also was a great philosopher who was deeply aware that 'he' was different from this material body. He used to tell his friends that the body is just a covering upon the pure soul, the important spiritual dimension of the body. At the end of his life, when he was administered poison by his enemies, he laughed at them saying that they cannot even see 'him' what to speak of capturing 'him' or killing 'him'!

Best Solace for Self Management

In any management training program, to increase the ability or capability of a person along with his inner potential to the maximum level, people take care of developing various aspects of human resources like the Physical, Mental, Social along with the Spiritual. In the present modern training process, we find that the missing dimension is Spiritual, which is the most important aspect for proper management of any person and is intimately connected with the being or personality. Spirituality is the main parameter in having the innate values like peace, joy, love, tolerance, humility etc in addition to the innate power like self respect and very importantly in enhancing the will power of a person through meditation. Recently, through science it is proven that "spirituality is the sure solace for the self management in terms of control on self destructive behavior and habits".

Patrick Glynn of George Washington University writes about the following points in his book on God.

(i) Those people who don't attend the religious or spiritual meetings are four times more prone to suicide than those who attend such meetings frequently.

(ii) People who have religious commitment are found to have negativity towards suicide

(iii) Lack of religious meetings attendance has been found to be the single best predictor of suicide rates, even than unemployment.

The American Journal of Epidemiology reports that the suicide risk among the middle aged people is 3 to 6 times higher among the nonreligious people than the one's who are religiously active. In addition, the studies by the West Virginia University scientists in Morgantown have reported in the American Journal for Health Promotion during 2001 that the spiritual practices like meditation, prayers and chanting of the Holy names of the Lord engender in improved mental health which is the main thing which is lacking in the present youth which is considered to be the main cause for the suicides. Therefore, the heart of self management is how to equip oneself to the technique of self empowerment so that they better manage the inner organization as a means for more effective leadership of the external organization.

Need of Self Empowerment in Modern Day Scenario

For the present day modern man, here are some of the inevitable life styles or daily circumstances, which are necessitating the human beings to the process of self empowerment on regular basis.

(i) Increased Work Pressure: The work pressure puts unbearable strain on everyone and also on relationships at home. In general due to high working pressures, the health deteriorates, self confidence falls and stress level rises. Sometimes people carry their family problems to office and fill their minds with anxiety, whereas some others carry the office to home and download the anger on family members. It is not an exaggeration that now-a-days top cadre management people with the intention of capturing the market works day and night hardly allocating time for their spouse and children. In due course of time, they become like a constantly running worn out hot machine, fit to be sent for overhauling to a costly doctor.

(ii) Team workmanship: Due to the process of globalization, it is becoming important for the top cadre managerial people like entrepreneurs, managers, and CEOs of many companies to produce their products at a lesser price within a short span of time but still maintaining the quality of the item. To meet such a requirement in a cut throat competition, the top leaders of any organization have to concentrate on the ability to empower its employees in keeping them satisfied as much as possible. For such a purpose, the leader should have good character and must be able to create a team spirit and the power of co-operation among the employees. Hence, as a role model the leader has to inspire all the employees for co-operation with others in the company which will be possible only when he himself is able to co-operate well with all employees of the organization. Now-a-days, due to involvement of time, money and energy, the process of team spirit is becoming more and more important. Team workmanship needs a common goal and in seeing the specialty of each member of the team along with their distinctive contribution for achieving the final goal of the project. A true leader is attuned to people's needs and the resolution of conflicts among the team members so that a good team workmanship gets developed in the organization.

(iii) Being loyal to the Company: Now-a-days, the companies are facing the problem of loyalty to their company by their employers. Many modern day corporations create insecure atmosphere among the employers. Some companies are using the employees just for the production purpose and do not care for them in any human way whenever they does not need their contribution. Due to the process of downsizing in a company, on one fine day, the employees often find themselves suddenly without jobs. Of course, under such circumstances, whenever the employees are not cared for their sense of well being, they lose their sense of loyalty towards the company and simultaneously, they understand that they are not protected by their own company because their leaders do not value them. Therefore, keeping talent of the employees loyal to a corporation in which they are working has become one of the greatest difficulties faced by the big companies in the entire world. Hence, leaders of the companies are trying to find ways and means to keep the employees talent to their own recruited companies by protecting their interests, self esteem, creativity and the development of trust in the corporation's vision. To achieve such a ideal working atmosphere, the leaders themselves should exhibit an exemplary life style by properly managing themselves and should inspire the people under them in similar direction.

(iv) Focus on Relationships: At the ending years of 20th century, it is found that Japanese companies are more successful ones in the world even than the American companies, even though Americans had better schools and more facilities. The research made by American universities like Stanford University has found that it is because of the Japanese genuine mentality rather than Americans ingenuity towards their companies. In many of the Japanese companies, people have observed that their employers and managers work together in a better way similar to the members of a family. Therefore, the success of Japanese business was based on their closer relationships along with team spirit. Many of the business schools all over the world including America now teach that success in any business management is about 20% by the technique and 80% by the relationships of the employees in the company. The term relationship means understanding the people's needs and being able to lead their lives from the platform of strong character. The character of a person is related to possessing the good qualities along with the originality in exhibiting them to make the person different from others.

(v) Importance of Character: In general, character is who you are especially when others are not watching you and it is shaped by how we choose our everyday thoughts, words and actions. There is a wise saying that "with Character one can buy anything even what the money cannot buy. The major obstacle in building up the character of the person is due to getting caught up in temporary pleasure of life and also because of lack of courage to come out of it. Warren Bennis the distinguished professor of business administration and founding Chairman of the Leadership Institute at the University of Southern California expresses his view on leadership as: "Leadership is nothing but good character and it has got to do with who we are as human beings along with those factors what shapes us".

Successful Tool for Self Empowerment – "Working Smarter but Not Harder"

By analyzing the structure of any organization, one can understand that only 2% of the employees do smart work as like the leaders of the company where as remaining 98% do hard work just by following their leaders. It's a general finding that hard work doesn't pay much but people who work smartly will earn a lot. The major factor in the smart work by any person in any organization/ society / family is based on success of relationships with others.

It's not an exaggeration that success in one's profession depends on his successful relationships with one's seniors, peers and juniors in the organization. Therefore, one should realize that our success as an individual is related with other people who are around us. To understand this in a better way, let us take a brief review of those factors in our day to day life, which will show our relationship with other people.

- True warmth and love comes from the relationships we have
- Our examination results come from the teacher
- Interview results come from the panel of members in the interview
- The job security comes from our senior or owner of the company
- The status, recognition, name, fame comes from society where we are living.

Therefore, one can easily understand that anyone's success from beginning to end depends on other people. Hence, one should know how best he utilize his intelligence to be a smart person to get along with all the people in and around you, and have the basic requirements in your life not dreaming of many unnecessary things in life for which you have to work hard.

To understand it in a better way, let us see an incident happened in the life of Socrates. This great scientist and philosopher once was seen by his friends spending a lot of time in market visiting many shops and keenly observing different items there. The friends have asked Socrates sarcastically, "Even you have started feeling of nice shopping". Then Socrates soberly replied nicely in a matured way, "I am wondering by seeing all the unnecessary things that are available for the people to buy". Shopping is really a great experience for many people. In the present day of high propaganda and glamorous advertisement, the shopping issue has become an irresistible activity for many. Acquiring and possessing new items gives great pleasure for some time only and for many people that charm of newness fades down fastly. Wearing a new dress, travelling in a new car, staying in a new house all will make us feel that we are above the ordinary and are surely special. But after some time, the burden of maintaining these new one along with what ever we already have interms of time, energy, care and money makes one to realize the fact that "Everything I own owns me". It's an irresistible fascination to people to have many things in their life. If they have some, they want a lot. And if they have a lot, they want a lot more. Therefore, an intelligent and wise person will be smart enough to decide what are the basic requirements for his life and will procure them only rather than procuring many more things thinking that they are necessary for which he has to work hard.

Self Control to Achieve the Will Power

In general, the art of Self Control boosts our Will Power along with Concentration and Memory. The will power of a person is the powers by virtue of which one can make his mind do what he wish to do. People in general thinks that it is easy to develop will-power, but it is not as easy as it is often spoken in seminars. Let us take an example of the technique for reducing the weight of a person as per the famous management consultant Sharu Rangnekar. He suggests that anyone who wants to reduce his weight has to shake his head from left to right whenever the tasty and fatty food is being offered to them. It seems so easy, but we have to remember this principle of shaking the head from left to right has to be executed when you are offered to have nice items like ice-cream, chocolates, fried stuff and sweets etc.

To understand the power of will power or mind power, let us take the example of a natural product i.e. water, which tries to flow from higher level to lower level. But only when we store it at a higher level by pumping it in to a water tank, against the natural gravitational forces, it develops the power to rush through the pipes and reach us whenever we want to have it.

Similarly, whenever there is a flood coming to a place without any restraint, it inundates anything which comes in its way like houses, trees, cattle, human beings and causes a big havoc for the entire living beings. When the same mass of water takes upon itself in between two restraints called banks, it gets momentum and moves ahead. When that water body faces one more restraint in front of it in the form of a dam, it becomes a source for the welfare of entire society. The huge amount of water which is stored in a dam can be productively used in a regulated way for irrigation purpose along with the generation of hydro electric power.

Similar to the flood of water, the human mind also flows in all the available directions uncontrollably. Many times, it happens that when we are reading a book, our mind may desire to watch a TV program and when we are watching a program in the TV, we may wish to meet someone else outside of our house. Therefore, only by will power, one can give undivided attention to do only one thing at a time. Hence, one must control one's own mind so that one can make it do what he wants to do. A person who has trained the mind such that he can think of doing only one thing for a period of atleast an hour will have a great force at his command for the entire day or a year.

Therefore, when one put's restraint on his mind from wandering can attain the will power to render any work perfectly at a particular time. Though the terms concentration and relaxation seem to be two opposite states of mind, both can be easily attained by a person who has the will-power. If one has the will power, then he can concentrate on living peacefully and happily amidst of any small disturbances or so called problems in his life.

Stop Worrying and Start Living Peacefully

In the present world, there are number of reasons why and how people are worrying – may be about their health, wealth, friends, loved ones, environment, politics and present situation in the world. At this stage, in nature one thing that is common is "change". The nature of the world is everything gets changed over a period of time, and essentially the biggest problem is we want to control our environment but in actuality, we are not the controllers. Naturally, things go in their own way. We can try our best to influence the things, but ultimately things are out of our control. If any one analyses his own body changes, one can easily find the major changes like birth, youth, old age, disease and death – which is a natural phenomenon. So if you are attached to any stage of your life or to any thing or to anyone on this worldly platform, then there will surely be worries in his life. Attachment to anything in general will result in a worry.

As a civil engineering faculty of our institute, I used to teach the importance of foundation of a building to the student community. The foundation of a building although could not be seen externally is the part of the structure which gives strength to the building and is the primary one which holds the entire structure in the correct position in stable condition. Similarly in our human lives, our mind will be stable when it has a strong spiritual foundation. In ones life, storms and reversals may come, but if we have that type of foundation of inner fulfillment, we deal with the situation with a clear and practical mind and it surely does not disturb us.

In this world, we are like strangers in a foreign land. Here, what is foreign is our conception – thinking that I am someone that I am not. For example, one may think that he is his own body and mind, which may get unlimited reversals and ultimately the body gets old and it dies. Many times people will be saying "Mr. X has passed away" – who has passed away, the actual body of Mr. X is right over there idle. Then who has passed away is the atma or the soul, which is really the eternal object in our body. So going back home to our real religion and uncovering the secrets of our true selves is the way to come above all this needless worries of this world and find real fulfillment. Then whatever happens in our live can not disturb that fulfillment.

In the Holy Scriptures, it is said that "A person who is not disturbed by the incessant flow of desires – that enter like rivers into the ocean, which is ever being filled but is always still – can alone achieve peace, and not the man who strives to satisfy such desires. For example we can take the difference between a pool or pond and an ocean. Due to monsoon season rains, the pool of water gets bigger and bigger, but during summer season, the same gets dried to nothing. It is therefore found that the pool or pond is very much affected with the rains. However, if we take the ocean, whether it is monsoon season or summer season, its level of water remains the same. Then what is the difference between the two. The only difference is the depth of water in each of them. The pool of water has lesser depth and hence will easily get affected by the environment and circumstances. But the ocean in itself has enormous depth and hence on the surface it gets affected by seasons but deep down, it's not affected at all.

In the similar grounds, in our lives, we have to deal with the things of this world on the surface, but if you don't have much spiritual depth, it really can destroy or devastate us with anxieties and worries. But when a person has that required spiritual depth, can uncover the truth within, deals with the things on surface nicely, but nothing can change that fulfillment, nothing can change his love which is within himself. Therefore, spirituality is the important factor to make oneself peaceful and happy.

What is spirituality and how to be spiritual?

Many times in our lives we hear this apt word of spiritual, especially in connection with places, objects, food, books along with people's lifestyle and mood. Then one may get a doubt about what exactly is spirituality. The Oxford dictionary defines the term spiritual as of pertaining to, or of affecting the spirit or soul, especially from a religious aspect. As per the saying of an eminent wise person "One who seeks happiness internally is a spiritualist and one who seeks happiness externally is a materialist". So, these two words are distinguished from the basic difference of from where one is seeking happiness – is it in matter or in spirit.

The Holy Scriptures say "A person who is not disturbed by the incessant flow of desires, similar to that of ocean which remain still although so many rives flow into it, can alone achieve peace and happiness". For a person who runs after satisfying such desires, these two things i.e. peace and happiness can not be achieved in true sense. God is like an ocean of peace and happiness and if we can invoke the presence of God within our hearts, then all the materialistic desires will not have any power to agitate our selves.

Is Spirituality Scientific and Practical

In the present fast paced modern technically advanced world, one question surely arises "Is the spirituality practical?" But no matter how fast paced our life becomes, the practical purpose of all our activities always remains in getting happiness. This factor of spirituality reveals to us the best form of happiness – that can never be taken away from us. It is explained in the Holy Scriptures that as spiritual souls, we all have an eternal loving relationship with the all-attractive Supreme Lord. And by developing the loving relationship with the Lord and properly serving Him, we can relish the everlasting happiness. Ofcourse, the more we love God, the degree of happiness we derive will surely be more.

India, is renowned globally as the land of profound and peerless spiritual wisdom. The Vedic tradition offers a well-developed science of consciousness study and transformation, a science that has no parallels in any wisdom-tradition. The potential of Vedic wisdom to bridge the yawning chasm that separates science and spirituality today is expressed by some eminent people and scientists as given below.

(i)   The Noble Laureate Physicist Albert Einstein feels "We owe a lot to the Indian, who taught us how to count, without which no worthwhile scientific discovery could have been made"

(ii)   Renowned French Mathematician Pierre Laplace expresses "It is India that gave us the ingenious method of expressing all numbers by tens symbols, each receiving a value of position as well as an absolute value, a profound and important idea which appears so simple to us now that we ignore its true merit. But its very simplicity, the great ease which it has lent to all computations, puts our arithmetic in the first rank of useful inventions".

(iii)   Henry David Thoreau, an American thinker says "whenever I have read any part of the Vedas, I have felt that some unearthly and unknown light illuminating me. In the great touching of the Vedas, there is no touch of sectarianism. It is for all ages and nationalities and is the royal road for the attainment of the Great Knowledge".

(iv)   Noble Laureate Author Hermann Hesse concludes "The most precious jewel and marvel of all the Vedas is Bhagavad-Gita and it is its truly beautiful revelation of life's wisdom which enables philosophy to blossom into religion".

(v)   The world's youngest Noble Laureate scientist Brain David Josephson expresses "the Vedanta and Sankhya philosophy hold the key to the laws of mind and thought process which are co-related to the Quantum field, i.e. the operation and distribution of particles at atomic and molecular levels".

Indeed, by uniting reason and faith in a higher-dimensional paradigm, Vedic-wisdom can heal the wound that has torn the human brain and the human heart apart, and thus usher a new era of integrated, holistic development in the entire world's history.

Less intelligent people some times discourage the aspiring spiritualists by commenting that "if you become too spiritual, you will become too satisfied and lose your ambitiousness". We have to clearly understand that our present existence is two – dimensional: we are spirit souls in the animating material bodies – just like drivers animate their different types of cars. Let us take two people: one wealthy and great person having Mercedes Benz, but lost the way to his home (not knowing the home even) and is spending lot of his precious time in just furnishing and polishing his car. The other simple and intelligent person, who has an ordinary Maruthi car but knows the way back to his home and is heading with the available speed towards the same. Among these two people please think who is better?

Therefore, as intelligent people, let's choose to be spiritually ambitious. Then we will really discover our spiritual peacefulness and reawaken our innate love for God and really become truly happy. In our cultural context, the two point formula for happiness is as follows:

(i)   Materially, see those people who are below us like having lower salaries, smaller houses, lesser or simpler gadgets and then be satisfied with what you have (which is really more than what others have).

(ii) Spiritually, see those who are above us, investing more time in yoga and meditation and follow in their foot steps.

Many times, humanity will be thinking that Love for God or practicing spirituality is impractical because it directs our vision towards the other world – spiritual world which is beyond the imagination of the present temporary material world. But this other-worldly goal does not make one impractical, but rather builds the most solid foundation for living happily in this world. For example, if we turn on the main or master switch for a building, then all the electrical appliances within the building gets automatically turns on. Similarly, when we awaken our love for God, our love for all living beings automatically awakens. Then we realize that all of us are like brothers and sisters in the one universal family of the Lord. When we start loving all living beings, then we never think of exploiting them for our selfish interests or desires. Instead we get inspiration to love, help and serve each other which will create a culture of warmth, trust, service and make our practical lives joyful.

By following a genuine spiritual path, we realize that God is our greatest well wisher and whatever happens in our lives is sanctioned by Him only and it is for our ultimate good, even it seems to be all wrong to our vision. Without the realization of God's benevolent orchestration of our life, the unexpected problematic and disturbing events in our life often become impossible things to manage. But when you are equipped with the spiritual vision, we will not feel for such incidents in our lives, rather stable minded people take such difficulties as concealed opportunities for learning many new things and for the required practical growth. Thus the path of spirituality is really useful, practical, and easy and importantly results are very beneficial to the managerial aspects of an individual.

LEADERSHIP PRINCIPLES

Leadership

Everyone in the present day circumstances, has to lead group of people either at the family level, profession, society, nation etc. Hence, one should be efficient enough to become a true leader who can lead the dependent people in a correct way.

History of ancient Indian sub-continent presents stories of brave, intelligent scholarly leaders who led great and vibrant kingdoms effectively. These leaders could rule the country with wonderful civilization which had people of character, values and ethics. In modern times, many of us could hardly find any leader with a good character and values. In ancient times, although there is no special literature available on leadership qualities, leaders have followed the available ancient scriptures like Vedas, Epics and Upanishads. In the present book, leadership principles based on value education derived from Holy Scriptures is presented to make oneself to be a good leader who attracts people's confidence and enthuses people to live a life with character, loyalty and faithfulness.

Knowledge from the Holy Scriptures gives concepts regarding emotional intelligence and its effective relationship with qualities of good leader. A great philosopher, Goleman mentions the emotional intelligence as one of the important quality that help people in general and leaders in particular to succeed at work and relationships. A leader's emotional intelligence, plays a key role in the overall performance of any family, organization, society or a country.

Need of good leadership

Bhagavad Gita is generally considered as a Holy Scripture which widely discusses regarding ancient Eastern philosophy and it is one of the best literatures in the contest of good leadership. Norwegian philosopher, Guttorm Floistad mentions that leadership in general is considered as achievement of some goal with the help of or through others. Many modern leadership techniques deal either with fattening your bank balance or to climb up the corporate ladder and to control people's lives along with more power. But what about that type of leadership technique or principle by which we can make a serious, significant contribution to people's lives and to the world in general? Actual leadership means to be a leader who actually has a positive effect in people's lives – and not simply leading in such a way that you make a lot of money or with lot of followers. What really matters is the mark that one leaves in the hearts of people and in the world.

The present day technically advanced society are needs leaders who live selflessly, with character, truthfulness, morality and God centered life. Many people speak about leadership qualities like patience rather than impatience, genuinity rather than superficiality, compassion rather than neglect and apathy for the sufferings and problems of others and also to be broad minded rather than being narrow minded, detached rather than attached to the ego, self-content rather than falling victim to temptations of one's senses. Therefore, let us try to understand these leadership principles to become a good leader so that many will follow us.

Who is a leader or hero?

In general terms people brand any one as hero if he has appreciable good qualities, which are admirable and can be followed by society. In student life, a topper in class or who completes his studies successfully with good grades is considered as hero in the class. These toppers, if exhibit good behaviour and character can be considered as good leaders to lead society in right direction. In a society, there will be 10% of the people who are the trendsetters whereas the remaining 90% are the followers of these trend setters.

Leader is a person who can show direction based on the principle centered life to the people of a family or society. Leadership is not a post to enjoy but is the responsibility of person to concentrate on providing ways and means not only for material benefits but also spiritual benefits of the people. Every young person who is pursuing his studies now will become a leader in his professional life or family life. Therefore, one should know the basic principles on which he can become a good and great leader at all levels of his life.

When you become a leader, people open their hearts to trust you; they open their faith. In that state you can do the greatest benefit to those people's lives, but you could also cause greatest pain, anguish and devastation in those people's lives. So leadership is not a post to enjoy. If you wish to enjoy the leader post, then you will be a exploitative person and also a miserable leader. In modern times, the three basic motives for leadership are the desire for power, achievement and affiliation. But actually, the leadership is a very serious, significant responsibility of service to others. A real leader is in the spirit of service. And, in order to be a proper leader in that way, one must have knowledge of what is actually right and what is actually wrong. From history, we find Gandhiji's legacy for the freedom in India, Martin Luther King's legacy for the civil rights movement in USA, Tom Watson's legacy in the growth of IBM, Bill Gate's legacy in the software industry and possibly Narendra Modi's legacy in Indian politics are the best possible examples of legacies in their respective fields.

Scriptures mentions that for a good leader Knowledge is power and the great thing is not about having power but how you use it. Are you using the power in such a way that you gain genuine inner fulfillment and enlightenment, and improve the physical, emotional and ethical quality of others? Radhanath swami, an American spiritual leader says that a good leader is a person who attracts people's confidence and enthuses people with loyalty and faithfulness because of their relationship, whether the relationship is immediate or extended.

Foundation of Leadership

Foundation of a building, although externally cannot be seen, is the basic part of building that gives it strength and holds it up always with stability. Simultaneously, our mind will be stable when it has a strong spiritual foundation. Storms may come, reversals may arise, but if we as leaders have that foundation of inner fulfillment, we deal with a very clear and practical mind, and it does not disturb us. In the Scriptures, it is mentioned that "For him who has conquered the mind, the mind is best of friends; but for one who failed to do so, his mind will remain the greatest enemy".

So, one gets a question of how to develop the foundation of qualities that make us a real leader. From different types of books, one may learn and memorize some of the qualities and one may try to practice and apply them in their own lives, which is certainly good. But as if one builds a magnificent building on a bad foundation, it will stand for some time, but when the storm comes, it will fall, because there is no real foundation. Hence, one should build these qualities on a strong foundation: a foundation of integrity, values and ethics based on truth. Then, no matter what comes in our life, we will not compromise. When the foundation of our values in life is in harmony with laws of nature, we will live in harmony with eternal nature. It is surely possible with spiritual practices, by which we experience and realize the truth, by which we have a philosophy, a science, to convince ourselves carry on with patience rather than impatience, with compassion rather than apathy to other's sufferings, with integrity rather than compromising for some temporary gain, with forgiveness rather than grudge.

As such Good leadership qualities include patience, genuinity, compassion, compromise, apathy towards others along with broad mindedness along with detachment towards ego and temptations. One should live with integrity and learn to forgive rather than hold grudges. One would have heard all these things, which is the basis of leadership. However, great people who are in elite positions, who could really have led the world in incredible ways, have ruined their lives by just giving into temptations. Just because of one little temptation, one's career, reputation and life gets ruined. Therefore, unless one builds a strong foundation to build these values upon, one will not be able to withstand the temptations and the pressures of this world.

Six qualities of a true leader

By analyzing the present day modern technical education system in developing countries like India, the author proposes six basic and essential leadership qualities extracted from the sacred Holy Scriptures. And if we teach these principles in all schools and colleges, the face of the society and country in total will change towards the mode of goodness and will surely become a role model for other countries to follow us. These leadership principles which are given below can be easily followed by everyone at the educational level, family level and also at the professional level.

i) Character

Character is defined as the combination of qualities and behaviour that distinguishes him/her from others. In practice, ones character determines the potential, skills and leadership qualities in a family, society, organization or country. In general, we recognize the good character of a person through his qualities like Integrity, competence, love and care, vision, honesty, inspiration along with behavior which is respectable.

As per Bacon for a person   if wealth is lost, nothing is lost because it can be regained

If health is lost, some thing is lost because it can be restored

But   if character is lost, everything is lost, which is true.

If you as a human being retain your good character through out your life, then surely you will have proper health and if you have both character and health, then naturally one will be a wealthy person.

As a leader if you are not having good character, then on one fine day you may have to face problems because of bad character. If we see the life of some people like Bill Clinton and Richard Hadley who were great leaders in their professional life one as president of a great nation and the other as captain of a leading cricket team have lost all their name and fame because of lust or greed. Therefore, every one should follow their regulated life style and should not get addicted to wrong ways of life.

Scriptures mention about the possible types of human characters as Sattvic, Rajasic and Tamasic. Sattvic character means a person with qualities of good harmony and purity and is generally exhibited by wise and righteous people who are in the mode of good consciousness and Rajasic deals with people having passion to do the things differently and uniquely while that of Tamasic deals with people of ignorance like that of demons whose mentality is to render evil or bad actvities. These scriptures prefer leaders with Sattvic character – those with righteous, harmonious, inspirational and virtuous behaviour. These leaders will try for self realization about the absolute truth and knowledge and simultaneously try to share this knowledge for the benefit of human mankind. However, leaders in the mode of Rajasic think of only growth and expansion in terms of money, fame and reputation. Whereas those in the mode of ignorance, are generally corrupt and are driven by their own personal interests and may cause lot of discomfort and inconvenience along with causing damage to others, society or even to an organization. Hence, efforts should be made to train the young generation to inculcate the sattvic character to be good leaders in the present modern day society.

ii) Competence

Competence is generally considered to possess the required abilities and strengths for a person to lead a life rightfully. In general, one should have the required knowledge, skills and devotion to solve different situations that may arise in life. During the student life, one should be highly skilled in studies competent enough to tackle people, problems, situations etc. Every student should learn the best principles during their education to the maximum level and should be competent in their memory, presence of mind, thoughtfulness to become good human being and also a good leader.

iii) Confidence

Generally, Self-confidence is observed to be essential for one's success in life and without such confidence people are afraid to take risks in their lives. In similar grounds, the basis for the real self-confidence depends on the effort of person in fulfilling the basic criteria as mentioned in the Holy Scriptures but not on achievements of successes. As per these scriptures, one should be able to know the answers to the basic questions like who we are and what is the purpose of our lives? Further, one also should understand what we represent to ourselves, to our families, and also to the society.

To develop such a self confidence, one should associate with people who have faith in spiritual truths and follow spiritual ideals. When we associate with such spiritual minded people and when we hear about the histories of great personalities along with their qualities, it provides us the real self confidence and we wish to follow their example. Real self-confidence can be born in a heart that's simple, honest, sincere and humble. Heart that has confidence in the higher power can bring us to the eternally liberated state of divine love, and bring us glorious successes in whatever we strive to do with the proper ideals. That is the true art of self-confidence.

iv) Discipline

In general people have been trained to do things because they fear some authority, not because they follow any moral principles. A child was trained to do certain activities in the designed manner because he / she fears either the parent or teacher or any older sibling. Similarly, an adult may do certain things because he/ she fears some one – may be spouse, boss, policeman or any other authority and mostly not because he/she follows any specific principles. As per scriptures, everyone either young child or an adult should do things as guided by certain principles as mentioned in sacred scriptures. A person without discipline, will do any type of bad or illegal activity when no one is observing but the same person will not do the same bad or illegal activity when anyone is watching him. But a person with self-discipline, will not do any illegal activity even when he is alone in an independent room with all sorts of temptations because he is governed by certain principles. Therefore, when any leader succeeds in creating people with self-discipline, then we can avoid much of bad or wrong situations or circumstances that are prevailing in the present society.

v) Tolerance

We are living in a world of dualities. It's a challenge to adjust one's consciousness and maintain integrity while tolerating dualities. A coin has two sides – head side and tail side. If you want one side, you must automatically accept the other; they are inseparable. Scriptures describes how distress is inseparable from happiness; or success and failure are inseparable. It also says about "the nonpermanent appearance of happiness and distress, and their disappearance in due course, are like the appearance and disappearance of winter and summer seasons. They arise from sense perception and one must learn to tolerate them without being disturbed".

People like to adore great people, and people like to become great in their own way. But what actually is greatness? At this stage we may get a doubt on what is greatness. Can a person become great by achieving lot of fame, by becoming wealthy person, being a good singer or good dancer, having beautiful body, being strong or athletic or being heroic? The answer is certainly a big No. According to the universal principle of all spiritual paths, this one line succinctly describes what greatness is: **"One's greatness has to estimated by one's ability to tolerate the provoking situations"**. This is something very important to be understood by all human beings.

vi) Positive Attitude

The greatest power of human intelligence is properly utilized when, in whatever situations that come upon us, instead of simply reacting we make an intelligent choice of what is actually the highest virtue that we can achieve. One of the Holy Scriptures - Bible mentions a statement "Knock and the door will open". Every situation is an opportunity and It is also said that, "When opportunity knocks most people complain about the noise". Vision is to see the invisible, to see the positive possibilities in every situation that comes upon us.

For example, one may say that "Look at this rosebush, it is full of thorns", which clearly indicates that he keeps on grumbling about the thorns on the rose bush. But another person may rejoice saying that, "Look at this thorn bush, it has a rose in it". Here both of them are seeing the same thing, but they are not seeing the same thing. So, according to our state of consciousness, we have certain attitudes, and we will perceive reality according to our acquired attitudes. What attitude we choose to adapt to a situation is what will determine our consciousness and our whole perception of the world.

In the present day advanced society, modern psychologists approach the attitude of human being based on the idea of a biological and mental being. Therefore, they psychologically try to help people in developing a positive attitude and accordingly, to help people with their physical and emotional conditions. This may be helpful, but it will remain incomplete if they do not understand the spiritual dimension of life. Scriptures describe that there are eight basic elements in a human — five gross elements (earth, water, fire, air and ether) and three subtle elements (mind, intelligence and ego). Besides these elements there is a superior nature, which is spirit soul, the conscious life force within all living beings. The soul, atma, is sac-cid-ananda, eternal, full of knowledge and full of bliss. They also teach about the spiritual dimension of human life and its relationship with mental, intellectual, egoistic and gross forms of matter. It is the greatest and deepest science of reality. It trains us how to have a positive blissful attitude in every situation that can come upon us, even death. A really good leader does not see anything as totally bad. He knows about the bad because he does not just hide from it; he is conscious about it. However, he looks for the good opportunity even in the bad situations.

Bad Leadership – Enemies Within

God teaches universally how to purify our heart. However, in the name of God, some people create cruelty and demoniac behaviour among the humanity. From where is this born? It's not just people do the things; it's envy in the heart, that drives them to do these things. Although we have different platforms for reformations in the humanity, still we will find many people developing envy, pride, lust, anger, greed and illusion in people's heart. The best example one can have is what took place on September 11, 2011 in Newyork city and Washington DC. In the name of hatred and envy, many innocent people were brutally killed in one incident. In such times of adversity, all Americans were angry against terrorist and their demoniac acts. But inspite of the people's anger and hatred, some leaders focused on national unity at those critical moments and because of their efforts it is observed that the American Patriotism rose to great heights during that period.

Good Leadership - Unity is the Strength

We know a popular statement – United we stand, divided we fall. This statement is simple, yet so deep. It conveys the critical importance of unity. But how to create that unity? How to create a common center that we agree on in a world of such immense ego, competition, and diversity? This is a great challenge, because wherever there is unity, there is a great power and strength to create a peaceful situation in society. By the unified inspiration of all of us coming together, we can help each other to access a power beyond our own to actually overcome even greater problems.

The topic of unity has pondered, reflected, and pursued since time immemorial – how to create unity within this world? One of the greatest powers in all fields of life is unity. In the present world, there is a fundamental problem – there are so many diversified distinctions between living beings. Everyone has their own conception of their identity, and this creates a natural conflict amongst those who look different, think different, or act different. Practically, at every level of the world, there is reason for conflict. Even within a family, there's the older brother and the younger brother and that creates conflict. So, as long as everyone has their separate, independent interests, there will be conflicts.

Our great India, which has different religions, castes and sections of people had one man, Mahatma Gandhi, who unified the nation is an incredible way. He has shown what could one little old man, who had taken a vow of ahimsa, non-violence, do to the British Empire? At that time, the British Empire was the most powerful force on earth, but this one small, old personality had the power to unify millions of people and that unity compelled the British Empire to give up and leave this wonderful land. This great person Mahatma Gandhi expresses his view on the great Holy scripture like Bhagavad Gita "When doubts haunt me, when disappointments stare me in the face and I see not one ray of hope on the horizon, I turn to Bhagavad Gita and find a verse to comfort me; and I immediately begin to smile in the midst of overwhelming sorrow". He also mentions that 'those who meditate on this Holy scripture will derive fresh joy and new meanings from it every day'.

Gandhian leadership and philosophy were well appreciated by great leaders like Dr. Martin Luther King. In his autobiography, he states that "Gandhi was probably the first person in the history to lead a life with the love of God and could create a powerful and effective force on a large scale through non-violence to achieve the independence to India". The author further acknowledges that this Gandhian philosophy on non violence is the one which could achieve social reforms in USA.

Scriptures states that we are all inconceivably, simultaneously one and different from God. The oneness between soul and God is in oneness of love, and we are all inconceivably, simultaneously one with one another. We are of the same quality, we are of the same origin, we are all brothers and sisters on the spiritual platform, but we have forgotten that due to ego, envy, and illusion. So any good leader must bring unity among all the people by cleansing their minds from unwanted things so that they could realize the actual oneness despite all the diversity amongst ourselves.

Love means sacrifice and service. The art of loving creates unity which has unlimited spiritual strength, and that is the greatest need in todays world. Each one of us can make such a difference if we become humble, develop a service attitude rather than an exploitative attitude, have broad mind to see the oneness and learn to love all living beings. What a difference each one of us could make, and what a difference we could make if we are united on that principle.

Concluding Remarks

Practically speaking many people may get a doubt that in the present day technically advanced world, will this type of holistic approach based on Holy Scriptures can bring any change in the our lifestyle. But, to bring some change in an individual or a nation, people in the society should change in terms of their behaviour, character, and attitudes in addition to leading life with values, morals and ethics.

It is a serious or difficult situation for all of us to bring such a holistic behaviour among the people when the entire world is moving very fastly in a different direction. But just for an example, any fish doest not wish to move along the water from a dam or a reservoir rather it struggles to come towards the upstream side by swimming against the flow of water for a comfortable stay. Similarly, it may be difficult or struggle especially for the students to have values based life in the present day circumstances. But if they really desire to have true happiness and prosperity in their life, it is the dire necessity to allocate their time to imbibe the value based life style along with good qualities.

It is very important to note that consciousness of a person is the most essential parameter that can bring any change in our life. If you are confident at your consciousness level, then you are sure of endeavoring a dedicated effort in understanding the importance of having values based life. With such an effort there will surely be a great evolution of wonderful things at the consciousness level or a person which are to be given top priority.

It is also suggested for all the administrative authorities to introduce the value based educational system into their curriculum with a view of bringing the right understanding about their life style for all the young professional students of our society. Let all of us as members of the society in general and academicians in particular join hands in bringing such a life style which will bring true happiness and peace in our lives along with our family members and society.

INDIAN CULTURE

God has created the entire universe for a significant purpose. And it is impossible for the human brain to attempt conceiving the creation of this universe with its different planets and each planet having a different purpose and functionality. Of the various planets, the earth is very significant for its ability to support different living entities. The wise recognize the importance of this planet by calling her "mother earth" and try to learn many lessons from her. Although subjected to many kinds of harassments, our mother earth continues to provide the necessities for all living beings.

On earth planet we have many oceans, continents and countries along with mountains and other natural bodies. People could imbibe certain type of culture depending on the place and circumstances at which they started living. Traditionally, eastern countries like India, China, Indonesia, Bhutan, Japan and Thailand are revered for their philosophical soundness. It is this kind of philosophical back ground on which these civilizations have sustained their life style and their socio economic systems for several millennia. These civilizations have retained the meaning and purpose of life and its harmony with nature. And among all countries, India is exceptional for its socio-philosophical nature, Vedic culture and Sanskrit language along with its spiritual atmosphere, and has made a profound impact on the rest of the world.

Culture

Culture generally refers to institutions, activities, ideas and other objects that the people of a country consider precious, and as having value which include knowledge, belief, morals, values, customs and any other capabilities acquired by man as a member of society. In other words, culture tells us who we are as human beings, how we are more intelligent than other living entities, how to aim our human lives, our desired behaviour and it also contains the implicit rules by which the humans can live happily with proper life style. In this way, the culture refers to the possessions of people in the society, their rituals, beliefs, ideas, myth and types of music, dance, art and craft. And importantly, this culture is generally passed on from generation to generation over a period of time.

In the olden days, one's possessions, values, morals used to remain for a longer period of time. And any additions or alterations, even allowed at small doses could not significantly alter the basic life style of the people. But in the present times, any addition or alteration, could influence the lifestyle rapidly. Depending on the place where one inhabits, the cultural principles will differ. For example, if a person is living in western countries, he/she will be very much after wealth, individuality and competition with others. Whereas, according to Indian culture, the same kind of person may give importance for family, society, respecting elders rather than wealth; furthermore Indians still consider ideals like detachment and renunciation. Similarly the countries like Japan and China, although being advanced in modern technology, still retains their basic hierarchical structure.

In recent times, leaders in the society place importance on the issue of development without much regards to the cultural dimension. Many times the important culture aspect is either ignored totally or considered as a secondary goal of human life style and this is the greatest blunder that is being done by human civilization in the recent years. As such we should not separate the culture and human beings and their relationship should continue for ever without any break or gap.

India and its unique culture

India in its national language is generally called as "Bharat", which is derived from the Sanskrit word of "Bharata". The Sanskrit language is accepted to be the top most of all languages with uniqueness in its vocabulary and script along with meanings. The word 'Bharata' is composed of two words "Bha - meaning light and knowledge" and "rata - meaning devoted". Therefore, the word 'Bharata' means the place where people are devoted to the Lord got illuminated by the light of knowledge derived from great scriptures. This type of spiritual truth was derived from the Vedas since time immemorial. This knowledge has made the people of India and the country as one amongst great in the entire world.

In the previous ancient times, India was amongst the richest countries with its great cultural tradition. Christopher Columbus was attracted by India's wealth and was looking for a route to India when he discovered the American continent by mistake. It has been estimated that the total amount of treasure that the British people looted from India crossed £ 1 Billion by 1901 itself and if we take minimum interest rates along with inflation it should be over £ 1 trillion today!

The Vedic culture and civilization, historically reported very long before the birth of Christ, has passed on from generation to generation without any break till recent times. Indians could establish great Harappa culture in Indus Valley Civilization where in there is a detailed knowledge about anatomy, physiology, embryology, digestion, metabolism, genetics and immunity etc. The Vedic Indian culture is certainly the most harmonious one with a great blend of art, religion and very importantly its great philosophy. Indian culture consists of timeless tradition of pure thoughts, feelings, social behaviour and values which elevate the consciousness of its people and benefit them. In comparison, the ancient Greek culture, which is mainly based on military power, imperialism and Roman culture which had very little spiritualism, could not sustain for a long period. The great Indian culture with its perfect blend of art, religion and strong philosophical back ground could withstand all the foreign invasions and could retain its originality along with its traditional character to a great extent even to this day, amidst the dynamic disturbance from the western culture. Indian culture believes that leading a spiritually oriented life, and a pure character, without giving much importance to wealth, power and beauty, are the pillars of the actual progress for human society.

The unique aspects of our culture can be summarized in three aspects

1. It is the oldest culture
2. It is pure and of divine one and
3. It has contributed significantly to science and engineering.

The main aim of any enlightened culture is to elevate its people to their ultimate goal. And a truly advanced society strives not simply for providing the requirements of eating, sleeping, mating and defending, which even all animals and birds do. Human civilization's requirement starts with a philosophical enquiry about God, universe and actual relation and position of all living beings. Therefore, spiritually oriented civilizations throughout the world's history had practiced a realistic approach of life that catered to all the needs of an individual interms of physical, mental, intellectual and spiritual aspects of life while stressing one's responsibility to the society at large. And similar to other living beings, man also has to live with and by nature's mercy of our mother earth and nature. And traditional land based cultures stressed the respect and cooperation with the other creatures in and around us, our mother land and also the nature. People of such cultures sought to extract from earth only as much as they needed, and to give back proportionately as and when needed.

Support to Indian culture

At this stage, a question may arise in the minds of many as to "How can India benefit from modernization without losing her culture to westernization?" The answer is that to modernize India without westernizing her, it's vital that all Indians understand the glory and importance of Vedic culture which is the basis of strong foundation for its culture. Indian shastras contain totally four Vedas, ten Upanishads, eighteen Puranas and epics like Ramayana and Mahabharat and very importantly the great Bhagavad-Gita. All these Shastras contain prayers and rituals along with spiritual, philosophical, ethical, moral and value based principles. Any one who follows this culture is sure to have a pure character and a life style uninfluenced by any bad alluring elements of the present society.

The present young generation is very much getting attracted to western culture, rather than appreciating its own great Indian culture. Let us review the statements of some western philosophers commenting on our Vedic culture and its literature:

(i)   The German philosopher Johann Gottfried Von Herder mentioned the Indian culture as "The Brahmanas (not by birth, but by the guna and karms) in India are the spiritual intelligence of the country and have great wisdom and spiritual strength to mould other fellow humans with great qualities like gentleness, courtesy, righteous and chaste". In addition the author says that these Brahmins could make the people strong in these areas and when we compare them Europeans will appear as beastly, drunken or mad".

(ii)   Another famous German philosopher Arthur Schopenhauer appreciated our Upanishads to be "the production of the highest human wisdom" and further proclaimed "It is the most satisfying and elevated reading which is possible in the world; it has been my solace in life and will be the solace of my death".

(iii)   The French thinker Voltaire asserted our Upanishads as "I am convinced that many things like astronomy, astrology etc. have come down to us from the banks of the Ganges".

(iv)   Another French historian Jules Michelet felt that India is certainly was "the spiritual bomb of the world".

(v)   British historian Sir Arnold Toynbee says that "the cause of the present day worlds disease is lack of spirituality. We are suffering from having sold our souls to the pursuit of an objective which is spiritually wrong and also practically unattainable. Therefore, we have to reconsider the objective and if required we have to change it, and until we do this change we will not experience true peace and happiness either amongst ourselves or within any of us".

Our Vedic culture and philosophy which are embedded in the Shastras and Upanishads are perfect and are the basics of peace and happiness for mankind from time immemorial and are also needed for the present day society.

Indian culture in general gives the aims and goals for life that were very well defined and were refined over ages. Other tributaries and reformist creeds along with varied schools of thought have enriched it over long periods of time and its ideology is very much time tested. People called this as 'Hindu' culture - the reason being some foreigners observed such a culture across the banks of river Sindhu. Unlike other cultures, this culture is found to be flexible and willing to learn good things from other cultures, absorbing them to retain the same and then passing it on to the younger generations.

Indian people are generally are more tolerant of the troubles and inconveniences that come upon in their lives. These people did not ridicule the traditions of other foreign civilizations or any cultures. This uniqueness in the mindset and character of these people is the one which is attracting the western society to Indian culture. There are so many instances of foreigners visiting India for understanding and following our culture along with our philosophy. In 1970s one young American Richie Slavin from Chicago, USA travelled by road for years to reach India for learning the science of God. He went on to become the well known Radhanath Swami. His book **"Journey Home – the auto biography of an American Swami"** details his adventure in the travelling through England, France, Italy, Greece, Turkey, Iran, Afghanistan, Pakistan and finally to India. In this book author talks about the greatness of this country and mentions the great Indian culture he had observed here by staying in Himalayas and also in cities like Mumbai.

Vedic wisdom through the epics

Ancient epics like Ramayana and Mahabharata provide the necessary wisdom through the stories of victory of good over evil, along with necessary knowledge for the seekers of spiritual truth for leading a regulated life style. The appearance of great personalities like Lord Rama, Lord Sri Krishna, Lord Chaitanya Maha Prabhu and Lord Buddha in this Holy land made the people see and learn many of the qualities of these personalities and follow in their footsteps. In the recent past the birth of great sages and philosophers like Ramanujacharya, Madhvacharya, Shankaracharya, Bhaktivedanta Swamy Prabhupada, Kabir, Tulasidas, Tukaram, Guru Nanak, Chanakya, Mirabai and their preaching based on the Holy scriptures like Bhagavad-Gita could provide the necessary wisdom and philosophical literature for the people to follow and upload the Vedic culture.

Our country had a galaxy of great visionaries who could pave the way with proper vision for action to follow the actual goal of life. The secret of continuity of our culture over the past years is its broad goals set by the great sages who followed and preached them. These sages had their teachings based on the great epics, have always tried to bring harmony of the body, mind and soul in all respects. With their own lifestyles, they made it clear that spirituality is not meant for running away from the realities of life into forests, but can be practiced by staying at the same place along with one's own family members. That's the secret of the preaching's of these great sages. But in recent times, our political and social leaders have discarded or distorted our Vedic wisdom - the impetus and enthusiasm of our great country. In the recent times the levels of corruption and dishonesty have increased a lot in our country because people have lost their commitment to follow the basic values and ethics.

Indian Art, Music and Dance

Indian Art which is high in its elegance, consists of the great religious beliefs and standards the culture is following. The temples in southern India and the caves of Ajanta, Ellora, Khajuraho are the best examples of the culture and traditions that was being followed by Indians. The architecture of these temples, the monuments along with different types of sculptures, renders efficiency and greatness to the professionalism of the people of those times. Many times foreigners have felt the true awakening of spirituality in their hearts upon visiting these temples and spiritual centres.

Indian music along with the dance is remarkable in its concept and growth. It is developed based on definite laws derived from the Samaveda. The two major schools of Indian classical music – the Hindustani and the Karnatic schools - were world famous for their ragas and talas. Each raga is regarded as representative of a certain emotion and there are more than about 250 ragas that are commonly used. Different ragas are associated with different times of the day and seasons of the year. Importantly, the Indian music has a calming and inspiring effect on mind, senses and also the soul.

Indian folk or classical dances are the eloquent expression of ancient Vedic civilization. Classical dances of India are Bharat Natyam, Kathakali, Kathak, Kuchipudi, Odissi and Manipuri. The rasa (or the bhava or expression) of these dances through the postures and abhinayas are very unique in style and rhythm.

India's contribution to Science and Engineering

The great Indian culture contributed significantly to science and engineering. Scriptures like Vedas have laid the foundations for many branches of science and engineering. Let us try to attempt to learn these contributions.

(i)   Law of gravity - Before to Sir Isaac Newton, Lalla and Bhaskaracharya II (1114 to 1183 CE) were the first to speak of the gravitational force. They have concluded that "Objects thrown upwards will always fall back to the ground due to earth's attraction".

(ii)   Rotation of Earth – Before Copernicus (1473-1543 CE), Aryabhatta (476 CE) a brilliant astronomer and mathematician proclaimed that the earth rotates on its axis as a result of which we to have days and nights. Bhaskaracharya calculated the time taken by the earth to go around the Sun once to be around 365.258756484 days. This was well before the days of astronomer Smart.

(iii) Diameter of earth – Aryabhatta (476 CE) and Bhaskaracharya II (1114 to 1183 CE) calculated the diameter of earth to be around 7,840 miles. Scientists using modern technology have calculated this value to be 7,926 miles.

(iv) Distance between earth and moon – The text book 'Surya Siddantha' compiled in 1000 BCE, mentions the distance between earth and moon as 253,000 miles compared to the modern measurements of 252,710 miles.

(v) Space science – the British Orientalist wrote that "Aryabhatta affirmed the rotation of earth around its central axis and the theory behind the solar and lunar eclispses. Aryabhatta also affirmed some of the planets like moon are essentially dark and can be only illuminated by the Sun". In addition the Sanskrit Lexicographer Sir Monier Williams says that "Whatever conclusions we could arrive on first astronomical ideas in the present days is due to Indian's invention of algebra and its application to astronomy and geometry".

(vi) Navigation – The word Navigation is derived from the sanskrit word "Navgatih" and was observed 6000 years ago in the Indus valley. Similarly the word navy is also derived from the Sanskrit word "Nou".

(vii) Atomic physics – Before John Dalton (1766 – 1844 CE) the great Indian scientist Kanad (600 BCE) explained that objects are made up of atoms and the entire world is made up of five main elements - earth, water, light or fire, air and space.

(viii) Mathematics – The Indian astrologers Varahamihir and Aryabhatta could invent the number "zero" for their astrological work called "Panchasiddhantika". Without this number zero, the present day computers would not have been possible. Aryabhatta is widely accepted by mathematicians as the father of Algebra. He could define many trigonometrical terms like sine, cosine, versine and inverse sine with different wording in Sanskrit. Bhaskaracharya (1114 to 1183 CE) gave the methods for addition, subtraction, multiplication and division as well for calculating the square root. He explained the concept of infinity with examples in 'Beejaganitha'. Sages like Apastamba and Baudhayan (600 BCE) developed the right angled triangle principle before the Greek geometrician Pythogoras. Baudhayan (600 BCE) is the first person to calculate the value of pi (π) as 3.14. Sidhacharya (800 CE) gave the formula for the quadratic equation. Madhvacharya discovered the Taylor series of sine and cosine functions 250 years before Brook Taylor. He also discovered the power series well before Newton did, and also discovered the Leibniz series for inverse tangent, and power series for pi, 300 years before to Leibniz.

(ix)   Health or Medical science – the great Indian sages developed the wonderful health science 'Ayurveda' during the Vedic period itself. Charaka (100 CE) is known as the father of Indian Medicine. In his book 'Charaka-samhita', he gives information on a number of diseases including typhoid and cancer. The great sage Sushrut (600 CE) is known as the father of Surgery as he is the first person to operate on the human body. In his book 'Sushruta-Samhita', he gives details of 300 types of operations along with hundreds of different surgical instruments. He even developed plastic surgery and could attach a nose or ear or eye to the person with his experience and knowledge. Also sage Jivak is considered as the expert in brain surgery.

(x)   Aeroplanes / Flying machines – Sage Bharadwaj (400 BCE) in his book 'Yantra Sarvasva', related to mechanical engineering, mentions different types of vehicles which can run on land, air and water. He also mentions different types of fuels for the vehicles including wind and light energies. In the chapter 'Vaimanika', this great sage mentions features of aeroplanes like cockpit, flight control mechanism, rudder and other related ones. In other epics like Ramayana and Mahabharata there are instances where incarnations of God and his devotees used flying machines to travel from one place to other without the necessity of any kind of fuel.

(xi)   First university – According to the scriptures, the first university in the world existed in Takshashila (700 BCE), which was formerly in India and now is in Pakistan after the division of two countries.

Takshashila had more than 10,000 students for undergraduate and post graduate courses in more than 60 subjects and there were more than 500 expert professors (acharyas). In addition of students from India, there were students from other countries like China, Japan, Egypt, Iran, Iraq, Italy etc. The other renowned university that existed in India was in Nalanda, now in the state of Bihar, India. Nalanda university also had many students in different disciplines from different countries around the world. It had the distinction of having more than 300 lecture halls and laboratories along with research facilities. All the Indian universities were destroyed during the invasion by the foreigners.

(xii) Civil Engineering – The popular foundation technique of well foundation developed by the Indian engineers is used for providing deep foundations below water bearing structures like bridges, abutments has been adopted in India for hundreds of years. Taj Mahal near Delhi, which is one of the wonders of the world, stands on a foundation built using this type of technique. This foundation technique is similar to Caisson foundation which was later proposed by the French engineers.

(xiii) Sanskrit language – According to American author and historian Will Durant, India's sanksrit language was the oldest one (even before Hebrew and Latin) and is considered as the mother of all languages. It is found to be the most advanced and perfect language in the entire world. Its great vocabulary and grammer are better than even Greek and Latin. The great Indian epics Ramayana and Mahabharata were written in Sanskrit.

(xiv) Yoga – The great Indian sage Patanjali has gifted the art of performing Yoga. It's a process for maintaining the physical and mental health. The term 'yoga' comes from the root word 'yug', which is similar to the word 'yoke' and means 'connect or link'. Hence Yoga simply means unite. In the book 'Patanjali-yoga', there are details regarding many types of yogas like hatha-yoga, astanga-yoga, pranayama, asanas along with the most important Bhakthi-yoga.

(xv) Games – The most difficult and thought provoking game of Chess which used to be called "Shatranj" was invented by Indians. This game utilises more mental strength rather than the physical energy and further requires great memory and thinking power. The origin of Martial arts took place in Kerala, India way back in 200 BCE. Kung-Fu begins with the legend of Bodhidharma (Aka Ta Mo) who travelled from India to China during 500 CE.

Therefore, let us appreciate the greatness and glory of India and that of Indians and India's culture. This wonderful culture has lot of morals, ethics and values and by following them let us become nice gentlemen and ladies in our behaviour and character along with becoming dear to the God through spirituality. Please rediscover the glory of India then enrich your own lives along with enriching the lives of spiritually impoverished people all over the world.